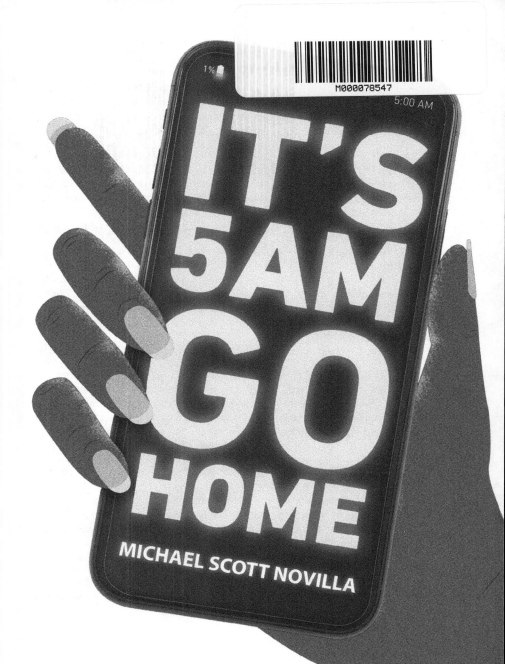

IT'S 5AM GO HOME

MICHAEL SCOTT NOVILLA

**Weddings, Parties & Events
So Good, Your Guests Won't Leave!!**

"Michael Novilla has built a premier event venue and business, raising the bar in a competitive industry. In fact, two of the best nights of my life were spent at NOVA 535 – my election and re-election as mayor of St. Petersburg, Florida. Those milestones were made extra special because of the venue and the expertise and precision demonstrated by Mike and his team."

— *St. Petersburg Mayor Rick Kriseman*

"Michael's NOVA parties are legendary for both their enjoyment, and the world class service you get from the NOVA 535 staff. Anyone who is responsible for creating and running high end events should benefit from his ten years of experience in the space."

— *Chris Jenkins, CDO Symphony Group*

"I first met Michael when I moved to St. Pete from Los Angeles in 2007 and I was immediately struck by the style and vibe he created from a run-down doggie day care into the premiere magical event location for parties, filming, fundraisers and so much more. But beyond the incredible venue, Michael is a visionary and this book is a must-read for entrepreneurs, party-goers and party throwers! He is a true friend of epic proportions and defines "Dream It, Believe It, Achieve It!""

— *Forbes Riley, TV Host, CEO of SpinGym, Award Winning Author/Speaker*

"Working with Michael Novilla is always a dream. NOVA 535 a spectacular venue and it always impresses those who attend. Michael and his NOVA team are creative, professional and really know how to make things happen. I couldn't think of a better person or better place to host an event, shoot a film, have a wedding or any other crazy thing you can come up with."

— *Tony Armer, Founder, Sunscreen Film Festival*

"I've used Michael Novilla's event space for several of my corporate events and every single time I'm treated with professionalism, and urgency to my needs. Quite simply, the man knows how to throw parties! When my customers leave an event hosted at Nova 535 they are always blown away at the impression of the venue. It's classy but cool, professional but fun, and always way above the norm – like Michael himself."

— *Topher Morrison, Author and Public Speaker*

"Michael Novilla and his staff at Nova 535 take care of every detail and his creativity is astounding. Michael goes above and beyond (even when) "just" having a corporate party and makes it an event that lives on long after the last guest has gone home."

— *Deb McLean, Cox Media Group*

"I've hosted a very successful party at Nova 535 every year since 2012 and working with Michael Novilla has been an awesome experience. He is definitely very knowledgeable and experienced in leaving customers & event planners with "the experience of a lifetime". Thanks, Michael!"

— *Jeff Copeland, Community Strategy Advisor*

"Michael is the King of St. Pete parties!"
— *Matthew Stover, NY Times Bestselling Author of "Acts of Caine"*

"Michael's commitment to the arts has served as a springboard for some of the greatest talent ever produced in the state of Florida. The diversity and breathtaking atmosphere of his venue is the perfect backdrop for moments that last a lifetime. Michael's historic venue NOVA 535 is an incubator for dreamers that span from up-and-coming entertainers to serial entrepreneurs. When Michael gets involved with an event, the only limitation is the customer's imagination!"
— *Daniel Jefferson, Founder Got Jokes? Entertainment*

"Michael's vision and creation of NOVA 535 is a destination venue. Michael Novilla and his team were world-class in service, and he even allowed us to roller-skate on premise – inside and around an antique Model A Ford! Wow! We had a jazz trio, a rock band, and then a DJ – and, of course, he afforded us the flexibility to extend the party until 5 am so we could keep dancing! NOVA is the place for a memorable experience with flawless execution, as Michael truly understands how to conceive, plan and execute 5-star weddings and events."
— *Amy Miller, Consult Amy Miller, Growth Consultant*

I have worked with Michael Novilla on and off over the past 15 years. I don't know anybody else who has gone to the lengths he has to help others. Always with a smile on his face, he is easily one of the most creative and inspiring entrepreneurs I have ever met. Inspires me to do things to the best of my ability. I highly recommend reading anything this gentleman has put into print."
— *Tom Shook aka "Dood" WMNF Host of ZentripZ*

"Michael is the rare person who has not only attended hundreds of parties and events around the world, but has also produced them! He has a personal gift for making people feel special and the business grit to take care of the details. Amazingly, he always has his fingers on the "life pulse" of an event. For over 20 years Michael Novilla has been has been a great business consultant to me and now is finally sharing his how-to weddings and event hosting secrets! As he spent 35 years to learn his lessons, it's well worth your time to read this book!"
— *Drew Edwards, Trustpoint Advisors*

"Michael Novilla was born with drive, wisdom, and vision. A self made, successful entrepreneur. His groundbreaking business ventures have rocked our community. He knows what it takes to win, how to plan like pro, and he throws such incredibly wild events! We all need to inhale every word of this book!
— *Rhonda Shear, Author, TV Star, Comedian, Playmate*

"I have hosted and thrown parties on an international level for over 15 years and his venue is unmatched. It's both beautiful and wild at the same time!"
— *Doug Hensel a.k.a. DJFresh, Official Tampa Bay Rays DJ President & CEO DJ Fresh Events*

DowntownStPete.com LLC
535 Dr. M. L. King Jr Street North
St. Petersburg, FL 33701

Ordering Information:

Quantity sales. Special discounts are available on quantity purchases by corporations, associations, and others. For details, contact the publisher at the address above.

Orders by U.S. trade bookstores and wholesalers. Please contact **DowntownStPete.com LLC** at Its5AMGoHome.com

Printed in the United States of America

Cover Design: Shake Creative and Melissa Caban Designs.

ISBN: 978-0-9997502-0-9 (paperback)
ISBN: 978-0-9997502-1-6 (eBook)

First Edition

Thanks to my executive consultant, Keith Long, and editor Karen Rowe, for their assistance in the writing of this book.

Table of Contents

IT'S 5AM GO HOME

MICHAEL SCOTT NOVILLA

**Weddings, Parties & Events
So Good, Your Guests Won't Leave!!**

Hey! I'm globetrotting Entrepreneur Michael Scott Novilla, back home to St. Pete, Florida after 416 days of traveling around the globe. Literally, around the globe. So, *no*, it's not flat. It has beautiful curves, like my parent's DNA. Their DNA, blended with my own wide range of experiences, made me into the eccentric kind of guy I am today.

From puffing my first terribly rolled "J" at age eleven to Kung Fu training with Shaolin monks in the mountains of China, I find myself choosing those paths less traveled. Well, those paths converged on a sidewalk in 2005 with me standing in front of a turn-of-the-century structure, in then-not-so-beautiful downtown St. Petersburg. A dog kennel with a for-sale sign in the window. Truthfully, and literally, it was a shithole. I walked away at first, thinking it was too crazy even for me.

Later, I thought about the fact that my hometown lacked a quality venue where folks could gather to cultivate friendships and celebrate important milestones in their lives. I gathered up my savings and borrowed the rest (total investment: $3,000,000) and jumped head first into a unique vision of what this building was destined to become: a wonderful place for our community to gather and throw epic parties.

I purchased the building, and after three years of renovations, it turned out the old dog kennel still had some bite! She was built with rare red clay tile and had a footprint that today makes it unique in its new incarnation as a 5-Star wedding and event space. Since its debut, it's been recognized many times, including, "Best Place to Get Married," "Best Holiday Party Venue," "Best Swanky Events Space," and one of "America's 65 Highest-Rated Wedding Venues." It also won the "Best Blank Canvas" award, not to mention the honor of having one of the "Top 10 Best Restrooms in the US."

Today, that building, NOVA 535, is the number-one rated venue in St. Pete, Clearwater, and Tampa, known collectively to us as Tampa Bay. We throw parties that are so good our guests won't leave! So I am inviting everyone to check out my wild and crazy story, *It's 5 AM Go Home*. It's the story of how traveling along my own unique path has led me to create something even more beautiful than just a new building. It's a way of thinking that I've come to call "the NOVA Way." It's been a wild, entertaining journey of discovery and continuous improvement for me and the team around me. Reading this book takes you along with me on the NOVA Way, a path filled with wisdom and discovery, suffering and enlightenment, that is never ever boring. We will laugh and cry together, and when you've finished reading it, you too will be able to produce your own 5-Star wedding and event experiences!

Chapter 1

Get Your Hands Up and Fight!

I spent my eleventh summer on planet Earth hanging with my best friend Danny, my fellow St. Jude's Catholic School rebel-compadre. Catholicism was served up in those days 24/7. We had eggs and benediction for breakfast, Sister Mary's fried guilt buffet for lunch, and dinner at home with Father, please pass the fish—it's Friday.

Ah, the 1970s. They were a very different time. Danny's older siblings, Ed and Cheri, were hip and oh-so-cool. The way they talked, walked, and acted, you could tell they had it. They were in, as in influencers. They had their own fancy cars while Danny and I were still messing with radio-controlled toy cars in the driveway.

Know this: As eleven-year-olds, we had robust curiosity, perfect hearing, and nonstop motor mouths. We were bouncing off the walls, yap-yapping away, listening, learning, and absorbing a lot more than the people around us realized. Older siblings were our internet. We couldn't

Google "how are babies made?" or "what's that stinky stuff they're smoking?" or "how to be cool." We did the best we could and adapted to the times by listening like two flies on the wall. We wanted so much to be cool. Yet, oddly, at the same time, we didn't give a shit about it. We really just wanted to have fun. During every second, all day long.

Danny and I were inspired by the films of the day like *Animal House* with John Belushi. Still, older siblings were our main resource for getting into trouble, and in our minds, they outshined the Hollywood stars. We scripted our own pranks, jokes, and zaniness. We had our own network way before Facebook, Instagram, and YouTube viral videos. We had an endless supply of energy to try to act cool like our idols. When cool got us into a shit-ton of trouble, we would just laugh, giggle, and laugh some more.

For example, there was a "serious" incident when someone left a bucket of live mice in the school administration offices. They were squeaking and running around the principal's desk. I don't know who was more terrified, the nuns or the mice. There was another occasion when someone poured liquid soap into the Tyrone Square Mall water fountains (long ago torn out and tiled over). It took on the appearance of a sci-fi thriller when bubbles (of gray goo fed nanotech) spilled over the edges of the fountains and morphed into a foam monster on the floor. There were no cameras or smartphones to record the disruption for posterity, only human memories. It was mouth to ear to mouth in those days. That was how legends were created.

I often wonder, how wise are kids when they're teens? Not very. Which, come to think of it, makes for incredible memories. Danny and I were brothers from different mothers and genetically endowed with way too much curiosity to decline the opportunity to "spark up" and see what (cough, cough) happens next. We had an entire lifetime of experiences and thrills compressed between our adolescent years of eleven to eighteen years old.

When I hit my adult years in the late 1980s, I was entering into serious training as a full-contact kickboxer. The core principles were based on Shaolin Kung Fu. I was bored with weightlifting and its repetitious, mind-numbing routines over and over and over. Today, my workouts are just chest and triceps; someone, please shoot me. Not that I was ever thick, huge, or ripped, but I managed to achieve some decent strength. The fact is, though, I was limited by my genetic predisposition toward normal (thinnish) arms that hung like they were dangling alongside my skinny calves. "Bacon calves" and "bird legs" were some of the common jokes I endured. I even wore jeans in the brutally hot summers to hide my skinny legs. All I could do was laugh along with my gym-mates. But inwardly, it hurt because I was so immature then.

As a kid, I had dreamed about getting cast in a film as the lead character with massive biceps, screaming, "Get to the chopper!" I was transfixed by comic books with those ads on the back page promising to make guys like me big and strong. They admonished, "don't be a wimp," and, "don't get sand kicked in your face anymore," and other nonsense like that. But at some point, I realized my genes were signaling that my biceps weren't going to be my path to fame. But I didn't give up. As a coping mechanism, I switched to following martial arts heroes on TV. David Carradine, who starred in *Kung Fu*, was Mr. Cool to me. I also idolized action heroes like Chuck Norris. Those guys weren't huge or overly muscular, but they were strong enough and definitely tough, so I could buy into that.

I began searching for a martial arts master. I hoofed it all over town, using the old-school, person-to-person method of asking around. I attended a few "introduction to martial arts" classes from wannabe teachers. The ones I tried out were either a joke or just not a good fit.

Finally, I found my guy. He was a genuine, full-contact, real deal martial arts master. Amir Ardebily is a fighter; a killer. His fighting model was a "no points" competition. Amir asked us with a grin, "Points? What's the point in that?" His gym was no *Karate Kid* movie fluff. It was brutal. Amir and I knew that out in the streets, you win or lose for real. It's the same in business, a stand-up comedy career, or with guys like me—hosts for live events.

Initially, there was no way I could be physically prepared for full-contact martial arts. The same can be said for my mental preparation. At that point in my life, my challenge was all about overcoming fear. I was a skinny, nerdy kid who got bullied from time to time. My identity was this funny, sarcastic smartass. I did know, however, that bullies avoid guys with confidence, and they devour fear. Fear is the mind killer. Just ask Paul Atreides, the protagonist in *Dune*. In the gym, I instinctively felt Amir's tough martial arts regime was the right path forward for me.

// —————————————————————

I must not fear. Fear is the mind-killer. Fear is the little-death that brings total obliteration. I will face my fear. I will permit it to pass over me and through me. And when it has gone past I will turn the inner eye to see its path. Where the fear has gone there will be nothing. Only I will remain.

—————————————————————**//**

—FRANK HERBERT, DUNE.

You have to be tough to succeed in business, right? Well, these martial arts fighters in the gym were tough as nails. I wanted to turn my ideal of being a street-tough kid into reality. #MindOverMind. Amir's martial arts gym taught me how to fight. His training was real and never boring. I intuitively felt that Amir's training was my best path forward.

Thirty years later, I can reflect on the takeaways from those hard-won lessons in and out of the ring. I remember the exhaustion, the pain, and the fear. Amir's unending— and at many times, brutal—lessons taught me how exhaustion, pain, and fear exist in your mind, not in the ring. It's all about mind over matter, commitment, hard work, training, and continuous improvement. Those were the key takeaways for overcoming fear. Amir pounded them into my brain, some days literally. Over and over, he repeated his simple philosophy: "Michael, good enough is never good enough."

Amir is still the best of the best. Just ask any of the monks he pinned at the Shaolin temples in China. Amir loves to tell the story about our trip there when some guy named Putin was visiting the temples. Yeah, *that* Putin. If you're ever out of coffee and need a jolt to your nervous system, try having a swarm of agitated Chinese Kung-Fu monks bang on your "dorm room" door (think in terms of a one-star hotel) early in the morning, demanding you give up your passports. We had to remain holed up inside the bare-bones dorm building, no explanations offered. There was a fair amount of confusion and concern. Fear can be the mind killer if you let it.

"Grab your headgear and mouthpieces" were words I loved, feared, and hated all at the same time. Fear, excitement, and nervousness were the uneasy feelings in my gut during Amir's classes. His greatest lesson was his unpredictability. I never knew what he was going to throw at us. I always had to be ready for anything. My ring opponents were usually bigger, stronger, and way more talented than me—and often dedicated to putting a real painful beatdown on me. Amir's brutal, full-contact lessons taught me how to try to keep my mind clear and how to always give my best.

It's the same with hosting 5-Star live events. They are, in their own way, full-contact. It is a "no points" competition when judging 5-Star events; either the event is fantastic, or you get a black eye. It can feel like getting punched, kicked, and elbowed just like in the ring. Fuses can be popping, or glasses may be breaking with inebriated brides screaming things you wouldn't hear on death row.

I have learned to smile at belligerent, rude guests, all the while thinking, *I would love to spray an entire can of foam insulation into this guy's mouth and do the world a fucking favor*. I deal with drunken bridal parties who skip out without paying their final bar tabs. I watch my team clean up in the wake of half-filled glasses, filth, ignorance, and rudeness. Occasionally, during an event, I face some of the meanest, rudest, most terrible monsters at a wedding. They remind me of the monsters created from the visionary mind of Stan Lee (RIP). I have come eye-to-eye with Bridez-illas and their evil masters, Momzillas.

Lessons learned while training with Amir have made me ready for anything, and like he says, being "good enough" is never good enough. His teaching created a framework that is transferable to my concept of a 5-Star event space business called NOVA 535. I applied Amir's discipline of continuous improvement, along with an attitude of never accepting "good enough" as good enough. My original concept for a NOVA 535 Art Lounge eventually evolved into something bigger than a world-class special event venue. NOVA 535 Unique Event Space is a brand and philosophy of its own: something called "the NOVA Way."

Thanks to Amir, my creation of NOVA 535 and the NOVA Way fills me with gratitude every day of my life. When I open the door and walk into the space I call "my baby," I am reminded of how thankful I am to be able to turn on the lights and juice up its entertainment systems. His training reminds me of the need to constantly push to achieve 5-Star outcomes. Our commitment at NOVA is continuous improvement. We target perfection while knowing full well that such a lofty goal is elusive. Perfection, after all, is filtered through the eyes and mind of every beholder.

Maybe that is why, for us, the NOVA Way is a way of life. So much so that it may be why my hilarious younger brother, Chris, occasionally and only half-jokingly refers to me as "Mitler" (Michael + Hitler). He thinks I am too strict in my desire to deliver perfection for every guest experience. Impossible, right? Just like putting a robot on Mars. We find ways to wow and delight our clients and their guests. How can we make our events better, more enjoyable, and smoother? How do we minimize errors? I carry forward the mindset from Amir's Academy of Martial Arts training. I have in my memory his voice imploring me, "You're only as good as your last round, Michael. Get your hands up and fight."

The pursuit of 5-Star customer satisfaction always brings me back to the time I spent in the ring. I experienced some terrifying moments against some of the best kickboxers in town. It was full-contact with fists and feet flying, elbows hitting me everywhere. One day, Amir announced, "Okay, you two guys are next." I felt my heart trying to burst through my ribs. My next opponent was that new beast, the guy who'd been pounding on everyone all week, and now it was my turn. *Gulp!* I think he'd been abused as a kid or something. In the ring, he fought like a monster, enjoying pounding on his opponents. And guess who was next? There were no weight classes at Amir's gym. It was you and whichever opponent Amir assigned you.

Damn, I thought. *This guy is a hundred pounds bigger than me. I am going to hurt for weeks.*

I had experienced Muay Thai poundings, grappling and getting my face pinned to the mat, and getting thrown around onto a floor that was unyielding. I got beaten like a rented mule. I remember wanting to yell, "Stop! Get the fuck off of me, dude." But I wouldn't allow myself to tap out from fear alone. The spinning backfists, opponents' kicks to my head, endless kicks to my shins and thighs—I learned to tough it out.

Amir occasionally started his classes with one thousand kicks. That was our warm-up. The chances of meeting the same person in Amir's classes more than once were slim to none. Most normal humans didn't return. So, here comes this guy.

He begins with endless and painful low kicks to my thighs and stomach. I'm barely able to stand up after the fight. Later, I limp across the University of South Florida campus and hear people asking me if I am okay. Do I need help? What kind of fucked up mind willingly chooses (and pays) to be brutalized several times every week?

I guess it's the same kind of mind that transfers his skill sets from a (somewhat) comfortable path of being a land-lord for the full-on insanity of managing and hosting live events. The NOVA Way is like running five live theater plays a week, each with a different plot, different actors, and unique, creatively staged sets. Something inside me seeks out challenges and punishment. Sometimes it feels like my path is a version of the stations of the cross. St. Michael Scott, Patron Saint of Tomfoolery.

In Amir's gym, opponents' arms banged against each other, then Amir beat us with bamboo sticks. Those three, four, or five classes a week took everything out of me and then some! The bamboo sticks whipping against my skin, inflicting quick, sharp pains that left marks that I called my temporary tattoos, which, for Amir's students, were painful badges of honor. The pain from Amir's sticks was more fleeting than the pain from opponents' elbows plunging deep into my muscles. Shin kicks were the worst of all.

Strange things happen in the gym. I started to enjoy the pain and somehow convinced myself to look forward to it. It's sick. Totally sick. Pain was never my real concern from Amir's training. I learned to handle it. After a while, I felt like pain was just a mental state that I could learn to ignore. My takeaway is that fear is the mind killer, so be ready for anything.

Amir called his training "conditioning." I called it exhaustion, and in Amir's world, it preceded sparring. By the time I got into the ring to spar, I was already spent. Fatigue crept in so deeply that it made me think about giving up before I could start fighting. I was already weary with salty sweat dripping off my hair and forehead, stinging my eyes.

Forward, I admonished myself. *Use every weapon, every ounce of energy, every molecule of whatever I still have available. Clear your mind, Michael. You can get through this.*

I hear Amir's command the second time: "Get your mouthpieces and headgear." The class forms a circle. My name is called. Back then, our ring was made up of all the classmates surrounding the fighters in a circle. Today,

19

Amir's Academy features a gorgeous, professional ring. I don't remember the first few rounds, because Amir left me in the ring as he swapped out my opponents. By the second or third guy, I was gassed. I remember when Amir called in his top student, Wayne Bingler, to fight me. In the world outside the gym, Wayne was a good friend and a super wonderful human being. In the ring, he was all business. He was also my Sensei Master. My teacher.

I knew Wayne had excellent control of his moves and never lost his temper. This day, I stepped in when I should have stepped out. Wayne unloaded a knee strike that found ground zero squarely in the center of my face, followed by a Superman punch. After that, I don't remember seeing anything, but I heard a gruesome, bone-crunching thud. Knee meets nose. I felt blood—my red blood—squirting everywhere. My head was spinning as I desperately tried to stay on my feet.

Backing up, head spinning, I realized something was wrong. I heard a muffled, "Oh shit, Wayne just busted Novilla's nose."

That was just what my Italian nose needed (not). More of it, all over the center of Michael Scott Novilla's face. Two Sensei Masters, Louie Izzo and Fernando Malagon (sadly, both RIP), helped to get me over to a chair. I remember thinking, *Glad the carpet is already red. I guess Amir planned it that way.*

Hosting live events is like fighting. Most of it can be executed perfectly, but all it takes is one wrong move. One misspoken word to a guest, one forgotten salad fork, one wrinkled linen—any wrong step can mean lights out. There is no second chance. Like a video game, you have no extra men left and no replay. Game over, head bowed in defeat. The sounds of Pac-Man dying. Quarters spent.

To stay at the pinnacle of the wedding and event space world, I apply what champion kickboxers develop after years in the ring: a positive, can-do-no-matter-what attitude. Amir used to remind me to have a win-at-all-costs mindset. After a while, I added my own personal wrinkle to Amir's approach. I remind my NOVA Way team to above all have patience. Lots and lots of patience. That wasn't and still isn't easy for me. It's a demanding business; success has to be earned one event at a time.

Just like with fighters, your output needs to wow and delight your customers each and every time. One bad event can knock you out like in Amir's ring and for real. Today, over a decade later, the NOVA Way is a proven business model and a respected brand in the wedding and live event industry. We are a crowned champion. Yet champions can and do get knocked out, and that's what terrifies and motivates me.

Amir's training model was to change things up, so I never knew what to expect when I walked into his gym. One day, several years into my training, he made a tiny fighting ring out of a half-dozen stand-up style punching bags. In such a small space, there wasn't any room for fighters to back up or dance around. It wasn't fun. Amir's command to start began with "mouthpieces and headgear." Like I said, he was always changing things up on us.

I'm not built like a fighter, and I don't like inflicting pain on anybody. That goes double for guys who are my friends. Like my good pal, St. Pete K-9 Officer Matt Regan. When I see him, he makes me think of Hollywood star Jason Statham. Matt and I spent a summer in Amir's gym beating the tar out of each other. In the days and weeks following our time spent in Amir's circle of pain, I hurt everywhere. I'm sure Matt did, too. Still, it was a great bruise-filled summer we shared together.

Years later, Matt and his lovely wife Aubrie held their wedding at NOVA 535. Whether I'm inside the ring, or during live events at NOVA, I have to be 100 percent focused. Not 99 percent or 99.75 percent—100 percent focused. That's why I get pissy when I watch my team checking their phones while a guest is waiting or something needs to be fixed. I (try to) put my smile and my game face on and to always pay attention to our guests. I don't want tonight's VIP to go unrecognized or ignored for the big event. That's all it would take for next year's event to get booked elsewhere.

Way before I ever walked into Amir's school and was attracted by the extreme discipline demanded of champion kickboxers, I appreciated the value of self-discipline. I was never a champion, but I did my best. I take pride in having survived countless hours and years of really brutal training there. I met some guys who enjoyed inflicting pain. I didn't enjoy hurting people. However, for self-defense, I could and would if necessary. As I've aged, though, I've swapped the brutality of Amir's ring for some soft yoga mats and endless beautiful women, all found down the street at my favorite yoga studio, The Body Electric.

Seriously, I have often benefited from one of the many important takeaway lessons thanks to Amir's gym: I know how to sense trouble. I have a Spiderman-like sense of avoidance. I use my inner (Stan Lee) energy to get out of sticky situations. At last count, I've visited eighty-seven countries, and I've walked down countless dark alleys and visited many dimly lit, alluring, dangerous, and exciting places. I will share a secret: Those places are where the best local scene is found. I love wading through groups of strangers, including thugs who are looking to rob, intimidate, or whatever. Amir's lessons have saved me more than once and, more importantly, given me the courage in the first place to walk down those dimly lit alleys just to see what's around that corner. I find the most amazing street art on the planet, in places partially hidden by motorbikes, loud, tough-talking dudes, and puke-covered garbage cans. Still, I like searching for that incredible local dish served up in one of those "neighborhood" cafes. I (usually) have the right instincts to turn left instead of right. I know how to avoid certain people and gravitate toward the more hospitable group, and sometimes, I make great new lifelong friends.

I've had my share of shots of illegal hooch and oil hash poured onto fat rolled greens. I've shared laughs and stories with some of the most "undesirable" of locals. I've had to navigate through hoods owned by gangsters and drug dealers. After what I've seen across the globe, I can sense who's full of shit and who to keep both eyes on. It's usually about respect at the alpha level and knowing what to say and how to say it. More importantly, sometimes survival is about knowing what *not* to say and when to say nothing. There's body language to pay attention to, and there's a right time to make eye contact. There's a time to show respect and humor while keeping properly tuned in with your street smarts. Keep the right distance so you seem mysterious, cool, and non-threatening, but demand to be treated as an equal.

It's a delicate balance traveling the globe. When 100-proof shots of diesel fuel start flowing, I move on. I don't want my mouth to write a check my body can't cash. Where did I steal that quote from? My mouth and brain oft times dance with three left feet and a broken strap.

I've learned how to pick up on native slang, navigate my way through unknown customs in different cultures, tightrope walk over razor wire, and walk away quickly when my eyes are bleeding and blurry. Have you ever tried to form words—cottonmouth in full effect—after eating native cuisine that made you chew and chew and swallow unrecognizable things? Lying directly into the eyes of some gangster's grandmother, telling her sincerely that you just loved her whatever-it-was (gag) is exhilarating and often terrifying. There are no headgear or mouthpiece protections in foreign lands. It's all level ten, baby. No saved players or extra balls. Well, lots of balls—just no credits left. If your flipper sticks, it's TILT, then lights out.

Looking back now, I appreciate how Amir's tough training regime was an extension of the family environment I grew up in. Not only was there the discipline of my Catholic schooling, but my parents ran their own tight ship. My father, Michael Francis Novilla, and mother, Leslie Jill Clark Novilla, demanded that we kids follow their rules. My father, an attorney, developed a well-respected solo law practice and ran it for over forty years. He was also a licensed pharmacist. He was known to us (thanks to my sister Julie) as Mr. Wills and Pills.

Dad was laser-smart, kind, and humble. He was someone I could always depend on. Julie referred to our dad, Michael Francis Novilla, as MFN.com. He did pro bono work for the downtown St. Petersburg Free Clinic. These days, I often want to call him to share my love. Then sadly, I recall that he's been gone too long. Life is short, my friends. Call your dad (and momma!) and tell them you love them.

Mom was an RN emergency room nurse and (still is) an extremely smart lady. My advice to strangers is, never try to beat her in card games. She reads daily, knocking out several books each week, and especially enjoys working on those 1,000-piece jigsaw puzzles. She met Dad when he was working behind the counter, filling prescriptions at the Pasadena Drug Store. Mom lived a few doors away in a modest house with her mom and brother. She had lost her father around the age of fifteen. They resided a bit north and east of the pharmacy, on the corner of 64th Street and 1st Avenue North. Her childhood home is still in our family now, owned by my wonderful Uncle Denny and Aunt Darlene.

Mom loves her three kids dearly, and after a decade or so spent patching people together from terrible accidents, dealing with dopers and shooting victims, carrying out sacks of injured flesh, there wasn't anything we three kids could throw at her that she couldn't handle—short of having one of our arms ripped off. She had firsthand knowledge of what real pain and injuries were like. Luckily, now her toughest decision is what she should do before going to bed. Finishing that juicy murder mystery, playing her baby grand piano (she is an incredible player!) or fitting the last piece into one of her massive jigsaw puzzles.

My parents had high expectations for me during my formative years, when I was enrolled in St. Jude's Grade School. Next, just down the street, was St. Pete Catholic High. SPCH was such an awkward time for me, though I did graduate with excellent grades, on time, in 1986 (just not from SPCH—more about this later).

I did the Boy Scout thing and earned Wolf, Bear, and a few other merit badges. I also earned points for woodworking when I built a downhill racer car. Dad wasn't a carpenter, so I taught myself the skills by whittling down a block of wood into the shape, mostly, of a car. I added wheels to turn it into a downhill racer. #CarpentryFail. I also occupied myself with soccer, bike riding, tree climbing, reading, hide and seek, kickball, and flying my favorite black bat-kite. There were yo-yo contests, and I bounced around on a squeaky, annoying pogo stick. If I needed rest, which I never did #NoNappingNovilla, I spent time roaming the stacks in the public library. It was the age of Hula Hoops, which, of course, I tried along with about a thousand other pre-internet time-killing activities like the slinky, Nerf balls, home-made mini-parachutes, and throwing Stretch Armstrong up into the treetops. #PlayingOutside.

I had a full-on hyperactive (mouth) schedule. One summer, my across-the-street neighbor, Becky, offered me her unicycle. After frustratingly scraping my knees and wobbling all over the place, I borrowed two brooms for balance from our garage. For weeks, I started out in the grass, trying to get the hang of it. I tried to stay on the seat long enough to ride past our house with no hands. That's what a unicycle is, after all: one wheel and a seat, no handlebars. The most I managed to do was stay on for a few feet each try. When Chris tells the story, he tells his friends "Michael never got his 'uni' to 'cycle.'" Funny, Chris.

In my adolescent years, spending money became the best tool to help feed my boundless energy. Dad, always attentive and helpful, picked up on my new interests— mostly video games, hanging at Tyrone Square Mall, and going to the movies. When he learned I blew all of his hard-earned bucks on these disposables, he took me aside for some coming-of-age counseling. He recited two of his favorite age-old truisms, passed down undoubtedly from his own father, Albert, when he was my age. He said, "Buddy, there's no such thing as a free lunch." The second axiom from his dad was, of course, "A fool and his money are soon parted." Dad and the family called me Buddy, which was short for Butt-in-ski. Because I couldn't control my mouth, I was always butting in.

Around the dinner table, Dad reminded me in his usual calm manner, "Michael, you'll never make enough money to buy everything you want." He wanted me to focus on making things happen myself, to learn the value of a hard-earned dollar. He wanted me to think, *Is this something of value and importance in my life, or just a(nother) silly whim?* He was always reminding me to stop and ask myself, "Do I really need that _____?" I miss those pearls of wisdom. And, no, 99 percent of the time, no I didn't *need* that _____.

Despite Dad's guidance, it wasn't long before I got the bug for the new 48K Atari 800. Yes, 48K. Not 48 gig. I was eleven years old, and naturally, I had no money, so I hit up mom. After saying no repeatedly and trying to deflect my endless cries of "please, Mom, *please, Mom!*" she would yell in frustration, "Go ask your father!" So, I hit up Dad. I waited for just the right moment, when he was relaxed, his work shoes off and enjoying his (only one per night) Brandy Manhattan on the rocks with an olive.

I presented my case about how computers were the future and so on. After revealing their hefty price tag, I got the hard "no." Then I tried asking for an "advance" for the $850 Atari, trying to collateralize it against future lawn mowing allowance earnings. Hearing a second "no," my remaining plan was to take his advice to heart. This experience turned out to be a memorable lesson that I'm most grateful for. #SelfReliance.

Dad was telling me that the only way I was going to get my Atari 800 was to buy it with money I earned myself. I hit upon the idea of starting a neighborhood lawn service. A smarter way to burn off my endless energy. Finding enough lawns to cut consumed me. Grass was on my mind (occasionally in my lungs) and under my feet. I helped Mom load up her massive 1970s station wagon with our trusty lawnmower and a can of gas so I could canvas the neighborhood for prospective customers. Amazingly, my business took off and grew like the weeds I was cutting and occasionally smoking. She was relieved to have my motormouth, which never ceased, out of the house.

Mom drove me to my new accounts that summer. After emptying countless bags of clippings and rolling up and then unrolling our orange extension cord—around and around my left arm she goes—edging those endless curbs just right, mixing gas and oil, pulling that fucking starter cord over and over and over when the motor was wet and tired, I *finally* got my first computer.

The ATARI 800 48K with BASIC cartridge plus dot matrix printer had a cassette tape as the disk drive. Yeah, it was that kind of old-school tech. We bought it at the local computer store, the Logical Choice, about one mile north up Park Street. The owners were sweet, always kind to their favorite "neighborhood computer nerd kid." I was featured on a local TV news segment named *Fascinating Floridians* twice; the store owners must have called into the network on my behalf. It was the beginning of a love affair with technology and the future. Love at first byte!

My teen years, not surprisingly, were my experimental phase. There were conversations about sending Michael to a drug program called Straight. Excommunication was also mentioned (just kidding!). There weren't too many of those kinds of conversations because, as things turned out, I had a good head on my shoulders, and curiosity was as far as things went. I am grateful Mom and Dad put up with their often wayward, motormouth son.

I came to some conclusions about drug use thanks to my experimentation. I think if people choose to use drugs too regularly, it's because they haven't learned to be their own best friend. It's a crutch. Maybe drugs are an attempt to fill that emptiness. Or it could be sex, exercise, or work. Filling an internal void with (fill in the blank) helps ease loneliness, and, in my opinion, loneliness is at the root of most misery in our lives. The first time I discovered the pain and misery associated with loneliness was when I fell in and out of love. Bon Jovi, baby! Hold on loosely, and don't let go (of that thought, or your 38 special, yet).

Throughout my school years, anytime I went to Dad with questions, his consistent advice was to figure out things for myself. #Learn2Think. He always kindly and relentlessly added, "Oh, and by the way, Michael, close the door behind you, turn off the lights, stop letting the AC out, and keep your room clean." They were his "cassettes." This was the repetitive parental wisdom that Dad and Mom showered us with—me, my sister Julie, and my younger brother Chris.

Dad bought a twenty-volume set of the *Encyclopedia Britannica* from a door-to-door salesman. His 1976–77 edition had everything you could think of in those thick-ass volumes. I'll always remember the gold trim of the pages. He even bought a double-stacked wood shelf to accompany the set, which he installed near the kids' rooms. I imagine that Dad hoped we'd look there first before peppering him with endless questions and curiosity.

Researching this shows that the *Encyclopedia Britannica* was started in Edinburgh, Scotland (a most magical of cities!) back in the 18th century, and it is the world's oldest continuously published encyclopedia. Many of you have no idea what I'm referring to.

Mom was way ahead of her time by creating a diet for us made up of all-natural foods. There were no sugary cereals in her cupboard. She read every label carefully and snuck protein powder into our shakes. She used carob instead of chocolate. We never drank sodas or ate junk food at 8212. I don't know how they can legally sell those toxins, especially with sugar, to kids. #YouAreWhatYouEat.

 What we *all* got hammered on was the endless TV marketing telling you to drink your (cow) milk. What a lie that was. Milk does *not* do a human body good. Perfect for baby cows, not for us. Thankfully, I figured this out, and my terrible psoriasis, intestinal gas, and eye-wateringly painful stomach cramps are all bye-bye.

Our neighborhood was populated with families who all seemed to share these same values. As a teenager, I knew my "hood" was a safe place filled with incredible neighbors. Down the street to the south and near the cul-de-sac storm drain, which had a big concrete cover (aka home plate), lived the Masters, Nancy and Charlie. Next were the Andersons, Bill and Judy. A little way down the main feeder road, 35th Avenue, was where you could find the Lewises, June and Ralph. Across from them were the Wagners, Meg and Linn, next to the future residence of my wild and crazy "brother from another mother" Charlie Mohr and his parents, Gigi and Hans. Just over a bit were Dr. Edward and his wife, Nancy Swanick, a nurse.

Our neighbors kept their houses and yards clean. They didn't let any of us kids get away with throwing trash in their yards, and we knew better than to display the slightest hint of disrespect to our elders or leave things (like bikes, skateboards, roller skates, etc.) lying around. We were reminded to use our kick-stands. Even scratching our bikes was frowned upon. Of course, it happened all the time, but things were to be taken care of. And even though it was quiet and orderly, we always managed to have a shit-ton of fun.

There was one family we all considered an exception that proves the rule. They were the Francatis, who managed to attract neighborhood frowns (this was the 1970s) when they became the first divorced family on the block. Their kids were older than me, and their house was a wild, wild west scene. Gerald, my buddy, was the youngest kid. (RIP Gerald. He passed from a faulty heart valve.) I remember the time Gerald set off fireworks inside their living room. I admired his bravado and wished then that Michael Novilla had those kinds of huevos.

Gerald had two older sisters who were gorgeous, and they attracted my young mind's developing fantasies. He also had two older brothers who were beyond wild. They were the super cool kids. I thought they were cool because they were playing with what I now hope were toy guns and racing motorcycles up and down the street, popping wheelies. These were the types of things absolutely forbidden by Mom. She had zero tolerance for guns and motorcycles; her life as an emergency room nurse was all about caring for people victimized by guns and motorcycles. There was no way she would let the three of us kids be anywhere near either of those. I didn't want her to know I even thought about touching a gun or riding a motorcycle.

The fun, adventurous, and cool Francati kids, alas, totally ignored me. To them, I was just a hyperactive, skinny, mouthy, and mostly nerdy neighbor kid who didn't seem to have much in common with them. Dr. Francati was an orthodontist and, luckily enough, I later became his patient. He did a great job correcting my bite, although he did nothing for my computer's lack of byte. My five years of dental procedures were expensive and captured a bunch of Dad's money. Many times, when I smile for a photo or while I'm flossing my teeth, I thank Dad for all his sacrifices, like five years of expensive braces; he was always focused on bettering his children.

I spent most of my time with kids my own age. Part of that time was devoted to hunting exotic animals. Me and my buddy, Greg Masters, did our hunting around Abercrombie Park about a five-minute walk from home, which was in west St. Pete. Greg was into animals, big time. When he grew up, he made his youthful interest official. Today, Dr. Greg Masters is a much-loved and well-respected veterinarian. Everyone knew from day one that Greg's destiny was to be a vet. We spent afternoons together catching snakes, turtles, lizards, tadpoles, insects, whatever. When our hands weren't full of critters, we were digging around the neighborhood's infamous vacant lot. Greg's sister, Kelly, occasionally joined our explorations. Their older brother, Brad, liked to sing crazy songs, and he developed a unique songbook full of funny lyrics. His niche was what I would call campfire songs, but he added a kind of Bill Murray-style narrative to them. The Masters were smart, well-mannered kids, just like their parents.

One of my best buddies became like an adopted brother to me. Ed Swanick was born a cool dude. He was into cutting-edge entertainment like Dr. Pepper, and he watched the R-rated movies expressly forbidden at the Novilla household. The 1970s were a great time for us.

His mother, Nancy Swanick, was an RN like my mom, and she tolerated me as her adopted second son. She was extremely patient, considering my limitless energy and nonstop motormouth. I knew when her patience was wearing thin because she would harken, "Michael, don't let the door hit your ass on the way out." She never failed to make me laugh as I made a fast exit out from her living room and onto my bike waiting just outside. I always glanced back at her to confirm with a nod that we both knew I'd be back tomorrow.

I spent a fair amount of time trying to get Ed and his younger sister, Jeanine, to play D&D (*Dungeons and Dragons*) with me. Ever seen a twenty-sided die? Who's the DM today? Creating quests and campaigns required lots of creativity. It was good training for team-building, role playing, developing creative thinking, and nurturing an active imagination, all while having a blast. A perfect foundation for a life of planning unique live events at NOVA 535.

I was very lucky to have the Swanicks as neighbors. Ed's dad, Dr. Swanick, moved out to the beaches when he and Nancy divorced. The doctor remarried a lovely lady named Carol, and they surprised me with an invitation to come along on a road trip that turned out to be epic. They took me on a two-week-ish car trip up the eastern seaboard to Philly and back. There's no doubt I drove them nuts. Seeing the country by car put the first spark of wanderlust into me, and it shines brighter than ever as I look forward to hitting my ninetieth country visited, real soon.

Our neighborhood had one house that represented mystery and adventure for us kids. It was a scary-looking 1920s mansion at the end of the street. It was believed that the house was owned by a giant retailer named J.C. Penny. The rest of the neighborhood was made up of single-story block homes, and there were only a few scattered two-story homes, so this imposing Spanish-style mansion captured our vivid youthful fantasies.

One day, I heard that a new kid on the block, Mike Lewis, had moved into that big scary place. Hidden behind decades of overgrowth and massive oak trees was enough mystery to fuel a hyperactive kid's imagination. Haunted? Well, in terms of a child's overactive imagination, you bet. Those thoughts got debunked after I met Mike.

In retrospect, I can say that my eleventh year was formative for me. I spent endless hours jumping with Mike on his trampoline in the mansion's backyard. We did double-bounces that reached over fifteen feet. We dodged spray from the lawn sprinklers that were set up just underneath Mike's trampolines so that we got thoroughly soaked. Another feature of my friendship with the new kid on the block was Mike's pinball machines. Yup, he had them sitting in their three-car garage. "Brick House" and other hip tunes of the day blared away on his stylish, expensive jukebox. The Lewises were my first up-close connection with people who had real thick money. I also spent time goofing around and joking with Mike's younger sister, Michelle, who got tagged with a nickname: "Sugar." She hung me with my own moniker: "*Nerd!*"

Mike's parents, Ralph and June, were cool, southern, big-money folks. Their world gave me the opportunity to get a look at real wealth, its creation, management, and benefits. June was super sweet and motherly to me. She kept fresh apples and pears in her kitchen. I think she hoped they would fill us up and limit the brews Mike and I might chug down later.

Ralph was a "Marlboro Man," rugged, good looking, and tough. My memories of him are forever associated with big $$. He made me wonder how it would feel to roll up to high school (shit, anywhere) in a Rolls Royce Silver Cloud. I thought about how cool it would be to drive around in a Lotus Turbo Esprit or an Excalibur (look it up). Those images made me say out loud, "Pardon me, do you have any Grey Poupon?"

I spent several years, mostly during the summers, working for Mike's dad at their expansive Sunshine Mobile Home Park. Sadly, we just lost Ralph, again reinforcing the reality that cigarette smoking isn't as cool as we thought it to be. I was actually traveling in Hanoi, Vietnam when I heard the news, and the shock created an unexpectedly emotional reaction even half a world away. I went to an outdoor cafe to vent, ordered a few glasses of red wine, and played sad music on my headphones. Then I cried like a baby.

That moment made me look at some of the cracks in my own life's foundation. I found a meme on social media that struck me. It said, "Tell those close to you that you love them. Life is short." Some parts of your life are centerpieces, and others are cornerstones. When they break, they make you feel like you've lost your own mortality. And then you begin to appreciate life's shared fragility.

The manager at Ralph's mobile home park was a character, a World War II vet named Jack Bird. He took me under his wing when I worked there. One thing I learned from Jack is that property rentals are passive income for owners like Ralph. He taught me that it pays to be proactive if you want to keep passive income flowing.

Jack was old-school and worked me as hard as he himself worked all day. My problem was, I didn't have anywhere to hide and fuck around. I had a few minutes for a lunch break, and aside from a bathroom break or two, that was it all day. There wasn't any chance to check my phone for texts every three seconds. And for a good reason—cell phones weren't invented yet. I worked all day, period.

Jack doled out daily work assignments. Sometimes, I worked on the truck that drove up and down the park's streets. He usually drove with Mike and me in the back. My role was to jump off and on the back bumper, all the better to pick up residents' garbage. Yup, I was a garbage man. But you know what? I loved it. I chose to work on the truck when I could rather than be trapped all day with the landscaping crew trimming tall-ass palm trees. Damn, my shoulders used to burn from reaching and struggling with that long, heavy wooden pole saw all day.

Jack laughed while watching me struggle during those first days on the job. I had to look up, squint through the sun, and target small bits of fronds to trim. There were hundreds of those damn little white flowers trickling down from the treetops through the air and into my hair, eyes, and mouth. All the while, I was focused on balancing that unwieldy, heavy, sixteen-foot-long pole saw, as it wanted to move me back and forth until I fell off the ladder. Ralph took pride in the park and modeled its landscaping after Disney World in Orlando. Every palm tree had to be perfectly shaped and manicured. I dreaded it then—well, mainly I dreaded that heavy-ass pole—but I appreciate and respect those experiences now. #Grateful.

I smelled like a sweaty St. Augustine salad thanks to the trimmer's gas/oil mixture, freshly cut grass, and a few end-of-day beers, which, when mixed together with the raging hormones of a high-energy teenage boy, made me forget what I was supposed to do. Instead, we were focused on women, how they looked, how they walked, how they kissed. Puberty in overdrive! When it rained, we couldn't use the mowers, which put us behind schedule, so Jack had me cleaning and painting everything everywhere on the thirty-plus-acre park. No details escaped the hawk-eyed Jack. He knew that "Hondo," his affectionate nickname for boss-man Ralph, also missed nothing.

My mentors were strict, disciplined, old-school, hard-working, detail-oriented men from the real school of hard knocks. Today's sensitivity awareness had no room to blossom in the harsh reality of battle-tested WWII vets. They were nice, kind guys, but real tough guys. No bullshit allowed. Ever. I worked nonstop all day. Nothing but real hard work. Nothing like the clown show I see happening in most businesses today. Pay attention to your customers, not to your IG feed.

That job taught me to operate and maintain machinery I was seeing for the first time. One day, Jack told me, "sharpen those mower blades, Mike." It was OJT (on-the-job training) for me to develop skills to meet Jack's high standards. In those days, there wasn't a "throwaway" culture. Jack used to say, "Those machines are built to last for generations, Mike." Yeah, sure, Jack. Instead of letting me buy a new mower blade, he made me learn to sharpen the old ones. I didn't think about it much then, but I was slowly becoming a young man—and a guy with some skills, no less.

I began to appreciate Jack and "Hando" Ralph as fountains of wisdom. One day, I asked Ralph about the new secretary in the office—or, in my hyperactive teen mind, the "sex-retary." His response? "Never dip your pen in the company inkwell." He then elaborated on the reasons why I should never ever noodle a lady who does the books. He was a giver of classic advice on how to avoid the toxic cocktail of mixing work and pleasure, which I fully appreciate now. It boiled down to being smart and thinking with your top head. He was full of other good, classic, old-school advice like, "Don't shit where you eat."

Jack was a WWII Navy veteran lured into the service by the promise that he could travel to exotic places. "Join the Navy to see the world," he used to say. He liked to tell stories, and I have to say that most of Jack's exploits are too raw to be shared or wished on anyone. One of Jack's pearls, the old Marine saying, "If it floats, flies, or fucks, it's cheaper to lease," certainly holds water today as I enjoy the fruits of Uber and Airbnb.

My takeaway from hearing his stories is that World War II was a horrific experience, especially for anyone who saw combat. He was in the middle of some bloody battles. I was endlessly surprised to hear the narratives of this sweet, kind man. We loved ole Jack Bird. He demanded that we do our work perfectly—which was how "he" wanted it done. Today, Sunshine Mobile Home Park is debt free and looks better than ever. The Lewises are smart folks, and I learned a lot from them; I can't thank them enough.

We the Novilla kids rode the bus to school. No helicopter parenting for us. A literal "fear of God" was entered directly into our souls for missing the bus. Belts and wooden spoons awaited our transgressive, tardy bottoms, and that was just the beginning of punishment. Fair to say, we never missed the bus. Our yellow steel box on wheels belched fumes and blue smoke when it pulled away from each stop with a new load of kids. My street, Colonial Lane, was the last stop and FOLO: first on and last off. Our driver, Mr. Montgomery, was a kind, older black gentlemen, who smoothly managed his load of white kids. He had a hand-operated hinged stop sign bolted on the side of the bus that stopped cars in both directions. As we ran out through the double doors, he'd smile and send us on our merry way. Word was, he had only one lung. I never knew if that was true–possibly just hot air or partial truth mashed into our urban legend buffet. Like the supposed spider eggs in Bubblicious, (that's why it's so soft!) or the nastier one about singer Rod Stewart.

Safely off the bus, we ran in all directions like roaches startled by a kitchen light. When I made it home, which was just two houses deep into our neighborhood, I put my school gear away in my room, did a superfast change of clothes, grabbed a snack from the fridge, and blazed toward the door before mom could snag me for chores. I could knock them out quickly anyways, and there was no escaping my household responsibilities.

I tried to finish my homework on the long bus ride home if I couldn't finish it during class. Why? It wasn't because I loved homework so much, although I did love school. It was because I wanted as much free time as possible. After school, the neighborhood kids gathered in our cul-de-sac, which divided the lawns of the Andersons from the Masters. That sewer lid I mentioned earlier rose up at the top-center (twelve o'clock) position of the street and was perfectly engineered for us to use as home plate for kickball, Wiffle ball, hide and seek, freeze tag, you name it.

Heidi Anderson, a smart, funny and really pretty neighborhood girl my age, attracted a lot of my attention. She and her brothers, Chris and Eric Anderson, hung with us. Our childhood energies for game playing were inexhaustible. Their sweet older sister, Heather, stayed mostly inside while the rest of us eked out as much fun as humanly possible.

When dinnertime approached, Mom looked for us toward the cul-de-sac at the end of the street. It was pretty easy to track us down because we were commanded to stay inside Colonial Lane and, of course, be home in time for our family dinner.

Dinnertime was—as my first love, a beautiful French girl named Frederique, would say—"like the chickens," meaning we ate too early, around 6:00 PM, which is typical of most Americans. The French and many Europeans eat much later. Try getting a good restaurant to even be *open* before 9:00 PM in many cities across the globe. During the turn of the century, my adventures took me through Spain, Barcelona, Madrid, Seville, and Figures with Drew Edwards, where we discovered "secret" restaurants that opened at midnight.

I knew I'd be in trouble if I had to listen to Mom yelling, "Dinnertime!" We knew to be home, washed, and ready for dinner by dinnertime—me, Julie, Chris, and the chickens!

I had a non-dinnertime strategy to hide out twenty feet off the ground in any one of our street's moss-laden oaks. I spent days and many after-dinner evenings in those treetops. I got a bird's eye view of the neighborhood. There wasn't any fear in those days, just adventures and excitement. Well, standing corrected, the fear of being late or disobeying my parents was one all-consuming fear.

Endless hours were enjoyed climbing from one tree to the next around the neighborhood, and, surprisingly, I never broke a bone or had an eye poked out. In fact,

I don't recall anyone in the hood who got hurt more than an occasional scrape or bruise. We were lucky. Countless things could have gone terribly wrong. I wonder if kids still climb trees these days. I don't see them, if they do. It's sad if they don't, although I eventually learned the hard way not to play around the oak trees' beautiful, flowing moss. The Spanish moss was pretty, but it was loaded with little red "chiggers" that made me itch like a MF.

The neighborhood was a kids' domain until the street-lights came on. Then we all timed things so that we made it home just in time to avoid getting grounded for being out when the streetlights were on. What a great sin that was.

One summer, Mike Lewis and I built a tree fort in his backyard. Unfortunately—or, rather, fortunately—it wasn't designed or built very well. When his dad, Ralph saw it, he tore it down and built a professional version. Ralph's tree house had a roof, a ladder, an entry door, and working windows. I now wonder if Ralph did it for us kids or because a shoddy model reflected so poorly on his otherwise perfectly manicured property. Spoiler alert: As a kid, I had my own private agenda. The first time I enjoyed sex with a girl riding up on top of me was up there in Ralph's tree-mansion. Talk about being on top of the world! Mike, fellow musketeer Charlie Mohr, and I offer our eternal thanks to Saint Ralph, Patron Saint of Mischievous Teenagers!

Whenever I could escape our Colonial Lane neighborhood, I took my bike for a ride a few miles south over to Treasure Island along the Gulf Beaches to visit one of my best friends, Danny Pugliese. His Entrepreneurial parents, Jim and Diana, founded a business called Omni Copy. I occasionally helped them out in the warehouse and gained an insider's look at the day-to-day operations of what was, in those days, a high-tech business. They had a massive building that sent shipments all over the South.

I accepted Danny's invitation to join him anytime he was helping at the warehouse. Our role was to carry boxes, clean and organize the inventory, and generally pitch in to do whatever needed to be done. The pay? Well, Danny and I spent days on the family's gorgeous '47 Motor Sailer, a Gulfstar aptly named *Elysium*. Also, Dan had a pretty older sister named Cheri and a super cool older bro, "Big Ed," who hung with us on the boat. For me, sailing was a showcase that sparked my imagination about the rich and stylish lifestyle.

Danny was one of the smartest and funniest guys at school. Sounds, noises, skits—think Eddie Murphy meets Richard Pryor, 24/7. A favorite destination for fun was the Treasure Island Fun Center. We were so silly and full of energy that it was nonstop laughter. I'd go there loaded with quarters for their games: Asteroids, Pac-Man, Donkey Kong, Star Castle, Pinball, and occasionally pool; assuredly, I spent every quarter I had. It was an all-day event for us at the T.I. Fun Center. When I ran out, I'd borrow from Danny, who always had plenty of quarters.

Danny drew up this funny bank book and would record when I'd borrow $5 or even a huge $10, which was a shit-ton of money back then. I'd always repay him, every nickel—er, quarter—so technically, Danny was my first lender. It's incredible that $10 was a massive amount of money then. Now, at least here in the United States, $10 is almost meaningless.

The sun setting meant it was time to get back home for one of Danny's mom's homemade dinners. Danny's mother, Diana, was 100 percent Chinese, and his dad, Jim, was 100 percent Italian. That made for amazing and exotic meals. When I walked in the door, before anyone could say anything, I announced, "Why, yes, thanks for asking. I'd love to stay over for dinner." After gorging ourselves, Danny and I went back to playing video games before transitioning into reading comic books like Stan Lee's *Spider-Man*, *Iron Man*, and *The Fantastic 4*. We were invested in making silly and hilarious noises long into the night in Danny's chic, super cool *Architectural Digest*-worthy house.

Their house became a second home for me, and I'm so thankful for these memories from an incredible childhood. The adults in our lives lived the American Dream and were good role models for being smart, hard-working, and living the life they created with their bare hands, minds, and hearts. Regrettably, Jim died soon after his retirement, which further baked in the valuable lesson of living every day to the fullest and living the life you want now. Live like you could die tomorrow, but plan, work, and expect to live to be a hundred. Don't wait for some mythical retirement. #CarpeDiem.

In the tight Colonial Lane community, I could always catch a home-cooked meal at one of my friend's houses. They usually had me help out while I was there, maybe cleaning up the yard, mowing grass, washing screens and windows, whatever was needed. I swept a lot of garage floors in my day and usually got a cheery invite to hang with them for lunch on weekends or in the summer, plus dinnertime year-round.

Of course, I made sure to offer to help set and clear the table as well. At home, my sister Julie and I put the dishes into the dishwasher and made sure everything else was put away before we left the dining room. I got reminders later in the evening to take the garbage out. Little Chris was a level-ten ninja at escaping most mealtime chores. He made sure to grab a few of the refrigerated items on the way back to his room. The word "refrigerated items" still brings smiles to our faces when repeated during family gatherings.

Our home, including my own room, was kept white-glove clean 24/7. That was mom's rule. When I was old enough, I acquired new responsibilities. I ran the clothes washer and dryer. Can you believe it? I did my own laundry at 10 or 11 years old. Weekends meant washing windows and screens, trimming trees, endless weeding around the yard, sweeping up, etc. I'm sure these family rules and routines hardwired a sense of self-reliance along with the Novilla can-do attitude into my maturing personality. Leave things better than you found them.

Thanks to mom and dad and the neighbors' value systems, it never occurred to anyone to ask for a "free" lunch. We expected to work for it. Money was hard to come by and easy to spend, so our parents worked hard at drilling in respect for its value and importance. My dad always said I could have anything I wanted if I got off my ass and worked for it.

Around the dinner table, Dad talked about how Americans were a blessed people. He talked up self-reliance (versus expecting a handout) and said, "Anyone can go down to the (free) public library, ask the librarian for a book, and learn about anything they desire." He said we have the freedom to make our own future. He told me, "Michael, don't make excuses. Create solutions."

His attitude is understandable. Dad worked his way through college to get his pharmacy degree by picking radishes at age eleven, then teaching and playing the accordion at college. After getting his degree, he enrolled at Stetson College of Law and paid tuition by working after school at area drugstores. He told me that learning how to think for yourself is more valuable than memorizing facts. He would have loved today's Information Age. We can Google anything we want to know, and, just as important, we can reach out to anyone through social media and have a conversation about anything. Of course, being able to understand what's on the computer screen and separate out fact from fiction involves thinking for ourselves. The internet leverages creative powers for Entrepreneurs and thinkers. I wish dad—"Pops," as we affectionately called him—was around to see how far we've come.

As I grew older, my prescribed path along our family's traditional Catholic altar boy ideals encountered its share of detours and zigzags. That's one way of saying I didn't always behave like the Boy Scout I was expected to be. . . . Not even close!

In my parents' home, spanking was the discipline of choice. I kind of outgrew that and discovered their next level of pain points were restrictions of freedom, which got handed out in increments of hours, days, and, finally, weeks at a time. I recall that at one point, I was sentenced to a two-month restriction. Going without a phone, TV, radio, video games, and, worst of all, hang-out time with my friends was a major bummer for young Michael.

I can sympathize with Picasso's Blue Period struggles, as I was certainly engaging in my own period of rebelliousness during those two months. I was an April Fool-born rebel, and as a result, I had lots and lots of time to contemplate my rebellious behavior while sitting alone in my room. It was a softer version of solitary confinement. I had literally nothing electronic for two months. I was alone with no one but me and my thoughts. I challenge you to go even two hours these days without a cellphone or a lit screen—no music, no video games, nada electronico. Imagine a quiet room filled with books. Shoot, try that for just two minutes. Back in the 1970s and early 80s, my school environment was technologically in the dark ages. There were no smartphones, and I had to walk for blocks to find a payphone. Then it cost 25 cents to make a call, and that only lasted three minutes; from there, the price went up. Back in the day, a 33 LP (long playing) record was the high technological watermark. If you want to know what a 33 LP looks like, you'll have to Google it!

I amused myself by rearranging the furniture in my room. I designed a system of strings and pulleys around the room that turned my lights on/off while I was on my bed. I also unpacked my Girder and Panel building set by Kenner Toys and constructed great, tall skyscrapers. And yes, my version of the Empire State Building had its own working elevator. I enjoyed a little socialization from playing board games with my hilarious, lovely sister Julie. Our two bedrooms were adjacent, so she could negotiate with me over whether to play *Monopoly*, *Risk*, *Life*, *Scrabble*, *Hungry Hungry Hippos*, *Operation*, checkers, chess, or any of an assortment of card games, including rummy, war, and Uno.

She was often victorious in our endless battles and today has become a beautiful lady and mother who is very smart and witty and always a good friend to talk to. We share the same sense of humor and make each other laugh with little more than a look or a word. I'm lucky to have an amazing sister like Julie. The love and memories we share are priceless. Julie's incredibly beautiful daughter, Sabrina Schultz, now Rudy Novilla Schultz, is off to college now.

I think Sabrina—sorry, Rudy—has our family's genes for big brains and zany wit. She also serves up stacked plates of the Novilla's flavored, deep dish sarcasm. She tells me I'm her third-favorite uncle. (She only has two. Ha!)

Whatever you are, be a good one.
Abraham Lincoln

Somehow or another, and despite my best efforts, as my rebellious teenage years waned, I found I had miraculously acquired an ability to think for myself. I began setting lofty goals and displaying discipline and even the fortitude to stick to my plans. I emerged from adolescence with a great burst of energy and a surprising dedication to becoming successful. I was always a voracious reader, and I still am. My greatest accomplishment was being able to create so many close friendships. My friends are people of every color, nationality, orientation, and style. Growing up, my parent's friends also had a diverse social network: black, gay, Jewish, Catholic, even Seminole fans.

My parents never used words that implied hate or bigotry. I never heard ethnic jokes, there was no demeaning of anyone, ever. Their kind of inclusiveness was not the rule in those days. Leslie and Michael Novilla weren't perfect, but they gave our family a solid foundation that we were all proud to call the Novilla home. Their rules turned out to be good for me. If I got mouthy—which was often—and broke the rules—which was also often—out came Dad's belt and Mom's wooden spoon to crack over Michael's backside.

The one deficit Mom and Dad suffered from was that they were never able to be my "how to party" role models.

They were rather tame when it came to that. I, on the other hand, found Tampa Bay a great place to party. And I mean *party*, party.

Our thriving ports are surrounded by endless world-class, powder soft, white, sandy beaches. The Gulf's warm, calm waters attract tourists from everywhere, including Europe and beyond. Tampa Bay turned out to be one great "party university," and I enrolled as a full-time student.

In one of my courses, I swallowed 50 cents worth of "game pieces" playing the infamous drinking game, "quarters." My good friend, Charlie Mohr, was one of the professors. The rules require players to bounce a quarter into a glass full of beer and then pass the glass to one of your tablemates to drink—the entire glass, without stopping. If your quarter missed the glass, then you passed the glass to the next player. If you are chosen as the drinker, you did have a wild-card option that was rarely used but available. While you were drinking the glass full of beer, if you could catch the quarter with your teeth as you gulped down the beer, you could then try to bounce that quarter—with your mouth—back into your glass. But before you bounce it back in, you refill it lickety-split. You then bounce the quarter you trapped with your teeth into the same glass. If your quarter makes it into the glass, you get to pass that glass to anyone you choose at the table. It's kind of like that "reverse" card in Uno. The rules are that you keep bouncing your quarter until you miss. Occasionally, we'd have to replace the missing (swallowed) quarters. So, fair to say, as I write this today, I'm worth at least 50 cents. Chalk it all up to my party games university training.

Fast-forwarding to 2008. My Lexus LS 400 lease was expiring, and, as it happened, the financial world's good times also were expiring. It was a nightmare commonly referred to as the Great Recession. You may have heard about it.

At that point, I began pondering my financial risk points while striving to be a greener, cleaner human being. Knowing the best way to grow and evolve was through change and struggle, it occurred to me that I could accomplish all three with one easy move. I turned in my car keys and decided then and there never to own another vehicle.

For one thing, driving after drinking even a small amount of alcohol carries far too much risk. In Florida, a driver is breaking the law if he has a .08 breathalyzer test result. That's only about one "real poured" glass of wine. I wasn't comfortable with that risk.

Everyone thought I was nutso. "Mike, WTF are you doing? How are you getting around, man?" Well, I had to rewire my thinking, which I did. Luckily, the future era of Uber wasn't too far off. Until then, it was bikes, taxis, left foot, right foot. Plus, bumming rides works just fine. Greener, cleaner, lower cost, and much lower risk.

I still hear Jack's Marine-born wisdom about leasing being cheaper than owning. Well, there's leasing an asset (like an LS 430) or just leasing the actual A-to-B task. Just-in-time transportation. It's a subtle but powerful difference. And when it comes to questions like "how much is parking" or "what's the price of a gallon of gas," who cares? Certainly not me!

Chapter 2

Party University

My classmates and I who were enrolled in "Party University" saw ourselves as young party gods. Special thanks are owed to my "professors": Mike Lewis, Michael Richards, Richard Fabrizi, the Whalen Brothers, Big Pete, Charlie Mohr, and many others I won't mention here.

Our study guides required us to learn to drink like titans, act like clowns, talk to any lady anywhere, and be able to react and adapt to whatever situation we got ourselves into. Richard pulled stunts I still laugh about to this day. He was so raw and so hilarious that you could never predict what he would do next. Luckily, we have grown and evolved since then, as we realized that healthy relationships had to be based on honesty, communication, and kindness. My classmates have all married, some more than once. I've remained on the other side of the aisle (single) and busied myself with making a living and globetrotting. I've come to be known as the "wedding bachelor," which sounds like a great reality TV show.

As students, we were night prowlers. My friends, like Charlie Kleinmetz, Steve Ware, "Farmer" Jay, and, of course, Lou "Cougano" Garcia, combed the beaches for brews and bikinis. Charlie would always promise to drive us home, full of buzz and bravado, and was always fast asleep on our way back from Clearwater Beach. We were wild, party-monster dumb fucks. Holy shit, could we drink. But at the time, it was fun. So many parties, so many ladies, so many stories. Laughing, cock-blocking, hot tubbing, skateboarding naked across Gulf Boulevard, and doing anything to avoid "captain interrupter." So much fun, night after night after night. I did most of the driving in my infamous Mustang GT, windows down, music blaring, acting out the role of a dumbass teenager. We had so many wild times that they are indescribable—literally. If I enrolled in Party University today, I would never drink like that again.

I became an expert at all the drinking games of that era: the funnel, beer slamming, drinking from a keg, quarters, and the questions games, to name a few. I really only lost one drinking bet. I met this guy at a party who challenged me to drink one six-pack of any beer I wanted in under ten minutes. I laughed, as my hubris got the best of me. We shook on ten dollars—which, as I previously mentioned, was good money back then. He said there was one caveat. I'd have to drink the beers one shot glass at a time. "Sure, no worries," I replied. *Burp!* I made it through about three and a half beers and had to call it quits. The air that goes into your stomach when shooting beers creates a most unpleasant effect. #LOSER.

While enrolled in Party University, I worked hard not to crash my cars. I had a hot '85 Mustang GT, which was the last year Mustangs were made with carburetors in them.

It was light and super-fast when a madman was behind the wheel. Danny had a new '86 GT with fuel injectors. Meanwhile, Lewis always rolled with a shiny new Corvette every year—like, almost every single year, a new Vette. Sickness. Lewis also had one of the earliest Alpine mobile phones, which was a beast compared to today's size standards. (Think portable house phone, yet bigger.) We'd meet ladies and enter their numbers, but at that time, there was no storage for a name, just those ten digits. It was hilarious calling weeks later, on a slow night, to see if we could gather up some ladies for a party. "Hello, is Lisa/Kim/Angie home?"

Richards bought and sold cars, along with some real estate, and was always smiling and enjoying life. He was also an expert salesman, charming and persuasive. Everyone loved "Big Mike," especially the ladies. One time, Danny and I drag-raced through the Treasure Island toll booth at well over a hundred miles an hour. I don't know how we survived. #StupidKidTricks. When I tell that story, I get asked, "Who won?" Looking back now, considering we're still alive today, we all won!

I've always been an early adopter. What I'm trying to say is that since age eleven, I've experimented. But only with women and drugs—sorry, guys. After failing terribly at our first rolled joint and not understanding hardware just yet, Danny and I got fruity. It's an old-school trick I learned at age eleven and have used over and over again since then. It's my favorite and safest solution in a pinch. You see, I've smoked weed from bongs, pipes (glass, metal, bone, and wood), joints, blunts, "Euro Cig" style, and, one time, sadly and never again, from aluminum cans. But from fruit?

My most recent old-school fruit-based smoking trick was with my pal, Steve Cook (RIP), in a moment of desperation at a wedding. Steve had plenty of weed on hand but no hardware. The wedding dinner bell was just about to ring with only moments to spare. Since we couldn't smoke inside and would be stuck at the table for about an hour, we got desperate. "One sec," I yelled, and ran over to the kitchen, returning moments later with a juicy red apple.

Core-core, fill-fill, puff-puff, cough-cough, pass-pass. Hmm? What? We laughed as we returned from outside, giggling as his medical-grade Cali powered flower kicked in just in time to dine at the wedding of his best friend (comedian Ron White). I lost many a neuron that weekend, but thanks again for the invite to Drew, who worked with Ron and Steve for about a decade.

The wilder Hollywood stories are locked up tight. Sorry, folks!

It's so sad we lost Steve. What a great guy he was. Tell your friends you love them while you can. And P.S. I still can't roll a blunt for shite; it's better to call my all-star pals "T" or "Jzon" for that.

Occasionally, we scheduled long weekends. Three days with nothing planned. Memorial Day weekends were perfect and always wild beyond explanation. A pal, Ms. Lisa Wright, is a lovely, hilarious, and brilliant Entrepreneur. A hard-working perfectionist, she is—a true hero in my book—who hosted the most epic, intimate house/pool parties ever. They were beautifully blurry weekends. We spoke to the gods, solved unsolvable problems, expanded our universe, danced to DJ Gazoo, and laughed and laughed and laughed. The atmosphere we generated on those nights was real, pure magic. We moved in and out of much higher states of consciousness. Our trips would have made Charles Dodgson (aka Lewis Carroll of *Alice's Adventures in Wonderland* fame) proud. We were struggling, evolving, blossoming Entrepreneurs.

On other occasions, if the stars aligned and we received glorious rain, a few key friends and I would forage around local cow-poop-laden fields in search of the most magical of spores. Our excursions were dedicated to my guru, Terence McKenna (the Timothy Leary of the 90s). My core picker pals were the hilarious "Emperor Hoanger," Sir Skeie, Carl (RIP), and Lenas, along with the exceptionally smart and funny "fung-guys," Chris n' Chris.

The mushrooms growing in our part of Florida look like they have a big nipple on top. They have a beautiful purple color below the crown and a ring around the stem. We organized our searches under very strict rules. Before gorging ourselves on magic mushrooms, there was a pause. We all had to agree that a shroom was safe to eat. If any disagreement was expressed, we'd throw away the shroom in question because of an underlying conviction that no buzz was worth dying for.

Another rule we followed was to never eat them until we got home. We never broke rule number one, but number two did get overruled occasionally. These trips were incredible and led to some of the most beautifully mind-expanding moments imaginable. It's been decades now, and I still miss those days. I still dream that someday the stars and spores will align once again, inviting me back into their universe of mind expansion.

Please don't live your life here on earth without at least once trying a magic mushroom (or three). Find a guru. Do it properly. Steve Jobs did acid, and who knows? That may have helped change the world. Think about that! Acid is man's feeble attempt at recreating the glorious mushroom. Enjoy, and thank me later.

My default hangouts during high school summers were the Nicklaus' Long Key Beach Resort and their beach bar, The Undertow. My high school friend, Paul Nicklaus, and his sister, Karen, put in some good words with their parents, Albert and Marty Nicklaus—along with their faithful dog, "Bunnie"—who owned the resort in St. Pete Beach. I was lucky enough to spend two of my summers earning cash by working at the front desk. I was professional and honest to a fault with their money and business, but I was happy to take advantage of the job in one respect: I loved spending time being part of the wild beach scene. I especially liked drinking at their beach bar.

The Nicklauses had not one but two amazing boats. The smaller one was a twenty-seven-foot Fountain racing boat, and the other was an incredible sixty-plus-foot yacht. Wow! Those times were beyond incredible and seriously wild. I wish we had camera phones back then—no way, Jose (Cuervo!).

I loved the Nicklaus family and appreciated their kindness, but I couldn't make enough money back then to fund the high-partying lifestyle to which I was growing accustomed. My good friends Paul and Karen covered for countless dinners, drinks, and boat trips. I was a frequent guest for lunches and late-night dinners at the family resort. While working for their parents, I made it a point to have my listening ears on whenever Albert and Marty talked about the hospitality industry. I truly enjoyed becoming part of their family, and I miss those simpler, happy-go-lucky days.

Working customer service at Long Key Beach Resort was fun and challenging. I took note of the maintenance and operation details involved for the more than fifty rooms there. I came to appreciate that being a manager required agile thinking. I taught myself how to problem-solve on the fly, knowing the watchful eyes of paying guests were monitoring me up one side and down the other. It was impossible to avoid being distracted by the ubiquitous college girl guests, and I occasionally found time to sneak into the resort's hot tub on a few of those occasions. Life was beyond fantastic.

At one point, there was a guy who dropped off his stash of adult entertainment videos for "safe keeping." They turned out to be cartoon porn. Yes, you read that right. Think caricatures of Bugs, Porky, Elmer Fudd, and crew, all done up 1970s-style animated porn. It was hilarious! He wrapped them in plain brown paper bags, and I had to keep my eye out for nosy guests trying to borrow from the shared stash of books and videos. There was one matronly, upper-class lady who I had to constantly shush away to keep her from peeking into those private archives. Cut me loose, grimy! (Ask Paul.)

The Nicklauses' business philosophy put the guests first. They were smart, kind, hardworking, welcoming people who were always smiling. Paul used to tell me that we were allowed to have our epic weekend parties, but on Monday morning, we had to be 100 percent ready to work. No matter what, when 9:00 AM hit on Monday, we were all business. All the monkeys had to be put back into the closet.

I appreciated the opportunity to be a fly on the wall to absorb some of the Nicklauses' behind-the-scenes planning for success. Long Key Beach Resort was a delightful place for me to learn all about the boutique hotel business. Albert's brother owned a bar just a mile north that had already become an icon for the beach community. Harry Nicklaus built it from scratch, and Harry's Beach Bar is now a quite fabulous name on St. Pete Beach. The place had a natural customer draw, since it was located behind their landmark gulf-front hotel, the Sirata.

It was nice to be best friends with families who owned the top resorts on the gulf beaches. One regret I carry with me from my party machine days was being too immature to express my full gratitude to the Nicklauses. They treated me like family, and I appreciate and treasure the time I had with them.

My immature teenage world was oriented around partying, and I took note when the first Hooters restaurant opened in Clearwater on October 4, 1983. Those days brought focus to the sweet chaos of MTV's annual spring break madness. The spring break scene rotated between Daytona Beach (three hours away), our own Clearwater Beach (thirty minutes north), and Fort Lauderdale (four hours away). And, of course, Tampa was also only thirty minutes away. We made the scene there at some of the ubiquitous bars and strip clubs along Dale Mabry highway, highlighted by the legendary Mons Venus.

This was the 1980s, and I was *out of fucking control*. If you weren't around here back then, you have no idea. We had stops at the Yucatan, Biarritz, the Big Catch, and Cowboys. We'd toss a twenty-dollar bill down on the bar during nickel beer night. That's twenty times twenty: four hundred beers. There was Rumple Minze (yuck!), Foxy's Café for bacon cream cheese toasted bagels and wings, plus all the 80s music we could dance to. #ThankfulWeSurvived.

When Paul and Karen's dad, Albert Nicklaus, passed, his Long Key Beach Resort was sold, so his kids focused on running their beach bar, The Undertow. Today, it's the number-one bar on St. Pete Beach. When I was working at Long Key Beach Resort, The Undertow was small and intimate, and it sported a hot tub. Decades later, it has become a huge venue, crowded with bikinis, volleyball players, and tourists from around the globe. It's best not to drive there. Do a rideshare or hop on your bicycle and enjoy a beautiful afternoon at The Undertow on St. Pete Beach!

 Young, Wet and Wild!

When I wasn't on the beaches, I looked for an outlet for my excess energy at home. Not surprisingly, swimming sparked our imaginations, and we were soon inventing new ways to pass the time. When variations of Marco Polo, tag, and retrieving all kinds of objects from the bottom of the pool got boring, I hit up a variation of Evel Knievel's motorcycle jumping stunts.

I was always on my bike, and often, when hitting our backyard pool, I'd ride through the garage or the back wooden gate and park the bike right against the house next to the in-ground concrete pool. One day, my brother Chris and our buddy, Chris' best friend from forever, Scott "Lork" Shirah, were hanging around looking for something stupid to do, and I pointed up at the roof. I imagined it to be like a huge ramp, just like stuntman Evel Knievel used to jump buses and cars in Las Vegas on his motorcycle. I said, "Guys, how about if I ride my bike off the roof into our swimming pool?" Upon closer scrutiny, I calculated that the slope was made for a perfect takeoff and would produce a three-point landing in the deep end of our pool. My imagination turned our roof into a runway for riding bicycles into a pool.

I used our wooden fence as a ladder, and, with the help from Chris and Scott, we got my bike up on the roof. Once there, I considered the science involved in this experiment before committing myself to a potentially bone crushing event. The roof had a fairly steep pitch—enough to provide speed. Screaming so everyone could hear, I announced, "I'm ready!"

Bombs away! Off I went, performing a perfect bike-riding "cannonball" into the pool and hamming it up a bit in mid-air for my buddies. Soon enough, my bro Chris and his bestie, (now Sheriff Deputy Scott), were doing their own cannonballs from on high. Chris, Scott, and I shared some great experiences that summer, and it occurs to me they are both fathers today. I've been thinking lately—fatherhood is something they've experienced, but I haven't. I am wondering as I write this if the fiftyish age mark is too old. Is it? It shouldn't be, as everything is (still) working fabulously!

My high school career at St. Pete Catholic experienced a hiccup with my sophomore to junior year transition. I was asked, politely but firmly, to leave.

I was finishing my Sophomore year, 1984, when I was at a SPCH pep rally. Naturally, Danny and I found our way over to the football field, then climbed all the way up to the top of the bleachers. The teachers were droning on and on while Danny and our crew were making wisecracks, laughing, and so on. #BusinessAsUsual. It was Friday afternoon, for God's sake. One of the Fathers was talking to the group and starting to get really annoyed. Finally, in a rare moment of broken control, he yelled out to everyone, "If anyone doesn't like it here, they can leave!" To which I replied—in what I thought was a quiet voice—something to the effect of, "Let's go."

And, whoosh. He fucking heard me.

I'm surrounded by something like five hundred kids, all yapping and carrying on, and I'm way up at the top of the bleachers. Yet, somehow, he heard me. Everyone stopped. The crowd went quiet as everyone turned to see who the Father was pointing at. *Gulp*. It was me. Talk about a walk of fame/shame. I made on my way down the bleachers and straight toward the school's office. Things kind of went south from there. On my way, the school officials heard more than they wanted to hear from my motor mouth, so I decided then and there I, too, had had enough. I walked out, never even reaching the office. I'd had enough of the fried guilt Fridays. Speaking of Friday, it was time to party!

I had never been in any real trouble before, but I had accumulated a bunch of behavioral demerits from going to lunch with older kids and doing doughnuts (that's pre-drifting) on the school's grassy campus. I was basically a good kid doing minor, rebellious things like motor-mouthing, sneaking around, having fun, burning off excess energy. I was never violent, never smashing or vandalizing anything aside from some torn-up lawns, and never stealing. From where I stood, it seemed I was trying to channel way more energy than the slow-motion high school educational system could contain. *Yawn!* I was doing a lot of joking around, as always. #ClassClown. Remember, I was born on April First–April Fool's Day. The Sisters of St. Pete Catholic decided there should be Nun-more of Mr. Novilla. Off I went to a new experience: public school. Wow, what an eye-opener.

I got off to a rocky start. The weekend prior to enrolling in public school, I talked some shit to the wrong guy at a party. His name was Paul, and we ended up doing business together decades later. He was a bigger, tougher dude than I was, and he clocked me–bang, right in my eye.

On my first day of public school, I was given the job of writing down student attendance for each class as part of my guidance counselor's elective duties. The thing is, this meant I got introduced to basically the entire school during my first week, all while sporting a huge black eye. I quickly got labeled as a mouthy sixteen-year-old new kid in school before I took my first class. It was an awkward time for me, as it is for all HS kids. Nevertheless, the combination of some personal growth and the exit from a school I never seemed to quite fit into created a new opportunity for a newer better version of myself. By my junior year, 1985, things started to come together.

1985 and 1986 were the years at Boca Ciega High School when I made many, many new friends. Also, the demographics were something like (generally speaking) 65 percent white and 35 percent black, as opposed to the 99 percent white and 1 percent black ratio at St. Pete Catholic. That, in itself, was another wonderful experience for me. Growing up on the west side of St. Pete, virtually everyone I knew was white. We had a bit of color at St. Jude's but not much. My parents had some delightful black friends, but we grew up effectively all white. Meeting, hanging out, and partying with my new black friends was incredible and it confirmed that people are people. Skin color is only that—a different shade of pigment. People are about how they act, not how they look.

My two years at Bogie, '85 and '86, were magical. I was on the Powder Puff team, where we ended up dressing up like cheerleaders. Danny Pugliese, Alex "Big Al" Brauch, Tom Fries, and I performed a carefully lip-synced version of "Piece of Your Action" by Motley Crue to the entire school. I forget why. I think it was a school-wide talent show.

Things are so different today than they were back then. Now, *everything* gets recorded. Everything has 4K video, high-res photos, likes, posting, permanent voyeurism. . . . Back then, we had only our organic memories. I mean, being able to see us lip-syncing to Motley Crue would be both incredible and terrible. Because just the act of observing something changes it. Ask Schrödinger's cat. Maybe we should have performed the more prescient Judas Priest piece, "Electric Eye."

In those two years, I got to kiss a bunch of ladies, drink gallons and gallons of beer—typically Michelob or Bud Lite—smoke weed now and again, and even try a wee lil' bit of blow. Didn't enjoy it much, I don't need more energy and paranoia, but the booze and green flowed like a river. As Van Halen would say, "dance, dance the night away!" Right here in Tampa Bay.

My nineteenth birthday party turned into a multi-keg, six-hundred-plus-person bash thanks to Steve, Kerry, and Ken from John's Pass Liquors and Deli. Mom and Dad were out of town, so a wild party event at my home was a no-brainer for yours truly. I considered it my Party University PhD thesis paper. I passed the oral exam in (almost) all other ways one can imagine. It was the first time my younger—and more athletic and better-looking—brother Chris got himself drunk. Chris was fifteen years old, and for some reason, he decided to run around in circles in the front driveway laughing and yelling his ass off. It was a truly epic and memorable party, sort of a take on the Tom Cruise movie *Risky Business* (1983).

One of my best friends, legendary Mr. Cool sportscaster Joe Pequeno, was in attendance. Joe always looked great. He was strong and buff—a real high school athlete. We all lifted weights then, and on Joe, it showed well. Biceps and arm thickness were the measure of the day, and he and our pal Big Brian always clearly "out-gunned" me. If you asked him, I'm sure he would remember the night well.

At one point, in the family room, I looked over and saw two guys drunk out of their minds, laughing uncontrollably. Next thing I knew, these dudes were peeing all over Mom's favorite pet love birds, which were flapping around like crazy in their ornate cage, disturbed to no end. *WTF?* They were trying to knock Mom's cute birds off their perch with piss streams. That was the moment it occurred to me things had gotten out of control.

Amazingly, with literally over six hundred people in and out, no cops showed up, and nothing major was broken or stolen. It was a wild, once-in-a-lifetime scene. #GratefulandThankful.

I do recall getting a mysterious and anonymous phone call early the next morning. It was a neighbor saying firmly that I needed to "clean up the mess strewn around the neighborhood," or her next call would be to my parents. Chris, Julie, and I found the motivation to protect our party secrets from the folks and went immediately into our ninja cleanup mode to keep the event our little secret. The funny thing is, our parents did have an overseer with us, but the scene just went so far beyond her control that she tapped out.

Something like twenty years later, the secret still air-tight, I finally told my parents at their anniversary dinner. By then, nothing about our wild childhoods phased them much. They laughed a bit, grimaced, and filed it all away.

Keeping secrets is the most difficult part of planning big events. It's really important to keep details cloistered and to reveal them just in time for your guests. This is virtually impossible since someone always blabs. A vendor leaks something about the venue settings, there's a cell phone butt dial from the caterer, the menu gets passed around after printing, an errant email gets posted on Facebook, or special entertainment details get mysteriously leaked.

I remember one extraordinary effort for one of NOVA 535's premier events to keep everything under wraps. Fellow Entrepreneur Van Fagan and his manager, Marie Crane, asked me to create a nice surprise birthday party for Rhonda Shear (Van's incredible wife, comedian, and *Playboy* Playmate) at NOVA 535. Rhonda is smart and sexy as a fox, a lady well known from her hilarious TV role in *USA Up All Night*. I read her book, *Up All Night*, and it's fantastic. What a life she's lived! NOVA prides itself in exceeding expectations for our celebrities and professionals who choose NOVA 535 for their once-in-a-lifetime events. Of course, Rhonda's party was marvelous.

(((Chapter 3)))

World-Class and Sexy

After graduating from Boca Ciega High in 1986, I enrolled in St. Pete Junior College, which, in a few years, became St. Pete College. Back then, we called junior college "thirteenth grade." At this point, I morphed into Dr. Love, the Party God. (Well, at least in my mind, I did.) Girls everywhere, booze flowing, weed whenever it was desired, fast boats, faster cars, gulf-front sunsets, all-nighters, hot tubs, the works. I did manage to score just well enough on the SATs, and the following year, I transferred into the University of Florida (UF) at Gainesville. Go Gators!

Back in 1987, '88, and '89, UF was wild and crazy. (1987 was the last year of "wet rush." I didn't join a fraternity, but if you were enrolled at the time, you would understand.) So much so that I forgot about my studies. I was way too into partying and having fun. I got good grades and continued to coast on through. Well, almost through.

Let's see. . . . On Tuesday nights, there were two-for-ones at Danny's. Wednesdays were three-for-ones at some place at the Oaks Mall. Thursday, we went to Central City. By Friday, who the fuck cared? Let's party! I had a connection for weed from a guy named Troy. Our phone conversations were down-pat. "Troy, it's Novilla; later." There were no cell phones, and when Troy picked up the receiver, he never had to say anything. I knew he was home, and he knew I was on my way over.

Bottom line, I spent way too much time playing at UF. I took too many opportunities to drink and hang out with ladies and gents passing around strong-ass weed.

I had always worked—ever since age eleven—and I started to look for a job in G-Ville. Poking around the job market wasn't fun. I asked friends for leads, and then I asked their friends. Eventually, my friend Aaron introduced me to his pal Frank, who referred my name to the owner of a start-up business. End of day—so to speak—I got hired by Gator Bumpers, who put me to work as a live game announcer and referee.

I used this new job's duties to hone my improvisational skills. No shite—Mr. fucking motormouth Michael had found a motormouth job. My duties were to jabber and blabber for fifty minutes at a time into a microphone and perform the role of a live game host and announcer. Wow! I thought I was the luckiest guy on Earth.

My job description at Gator Bumpers required me to master a different type of game: bumper cars. They had two teams of five cars each, five red and five yellow. Each player was given a Jai Alai shaped plastic scoop with a plastic white Wiffle ball to covet. (All guys my age can recall owning a Wiffle ball at some point.) The object at Gator Bumpers was to toss the ball up through a hole cut into the center of a basketball backboard, with a net just behind it. Players scooped up the bouncing white Wiffle ball while driving around the course in their colored bumper cars. Whichever car had the Wiffle ball was targeted for slams by other drivers from every conceivable angle. As the target, a Wiffle ball driver had to skillfully flick his wrist and shoot the ball through the tiny hole in the backboard atop a regulation-sized basketball pole. It was insanity!

The boss told me I had to think on my feet, but I was actually sitting in a comfy chair. What a perfect entry into the wild and often unpredictable world of the 5-Star wedding and event space business!

I learned live event management literally on the fly. It was OJT (on-the-job training) for many of the real-world skills that I was not getting at UF. The University of Florida is a great university. Top notch. You learn all kinds of things, but nothing I learned there seemed transferable to knowing how to operate a real business. So, while floundering around in business school, what I didn't know yet was that (in class), I was not really learning the real skills of a small business Entrepreneur.

This was how I earned spending money during college: working at a college bar and bumper car game center. There was endless booze flowing, ping-pong battles, free pinball, snacks, gorgeous sorority ladies, and folks proudly sharing the sticky, strong Gainesville Green. Luckily, I breezed through my classes in those years and effortlessly divided my time between class, work, and play—in reverse order.

My buddy, Mike Lewis, drove up from St. Pete to Gainesville and enrolled at a nearby community college. He pretended to be studying hard, but we were actually partying together. We spent countless hours banging around in the bumper cars, laughing, drinking, and having lots of fun. Life was one big game to me. Or, rather, it was one endless party of extra balls, free games, and no tilts—except for the bottles of liquor we were pouring down our throats. Yee-fucking-haw!

I had a "dealin'" machine for wheels then: my 1985 Red Mustang GT with 3x90 tinted windows. That meant no one could see into the car from the outside. I could literally be buck-naked smoking a joint, drinking bottles of Bud Light from a cooler with my current girlfriend, and if a police officer came by and stared directly into the windows at us, we would be totally in the clear. I was in full-on beach-mentality party boy mode. My hair was long in the back, I had a pierced left ear, and the only shape I was in (at this time) was party-ready.

Mike Lewis brought his dad's Lotus Turbo Esprit up to Gainesville. When we weren't at Gator Bumpers, we attracted eyeballs by zipping all over town. We spent one beautiful late summer morning in the Lotus driving up and down a quiet, smooth, and perfectly flat country road somewhere outside of Gainesville. We made a few dry runs to make sure the scene was set for a big finale. (They weren't really dry runs. He and I were slurping down Mich Lights, in the bottle, for fortification.) Suddenly, and without warning, Mike slammed his foot on the gas pedal full-on and took his Lotus past the redline at 100 miles an hour. Next thing I saw was the needle touch 120, 130, 140, 145, 150, 155, 160. . . . Holy shit!

That day, Mike touched 165 just as we ran out of road. Talk about white knuckles. Wow, what a thrill! I enjoyed the rush from the top-end burst of speed, but I was legitimately terrified that a squirrel or a dog would go jumping out in front of us. Family farms were all around. A fuck-up at 165 miles an hour meant game o–-*swerve*–ver. To this day, I have never touched 165 miles per hour again in an automobile. Try it if you dare. But it's difficult to find a live road and the right time to do it. You need a car to get you to that speed, a road that's flat enough and long enough, and the right timing, when there aren't any other cars, cops, squirrels, ducks–you get it. And finally, it helps to have a little luck to survive. It also helps to have the balls to push a car to that speed. Props to Mike.

Life continued free and easy until a "required course schedule" slotted me into pre-calculus. At that point, I hit a wall. Like Pink Floyd, I started seeing the dark side of the party moon.

I failed my first class ever, and I was stunned. I asked myself, "How could this happen?" What was I going to do? I said to myself, "Think, Michael, think." I had no choice but to buckle down and hire a tutor to get me through this rough spot in the road. "Be smart," I kept reminding myself. I checked out the school paper, *The Alligator*, for tutors and asked friends and classmates. Luckily, I found one of the greatest guys I've ever met: Drew Hudson Edwards. He advertised his tutoring business, known as Concepts Tutoring, in a professionally done ad. It was so cool. The ad featured a monkey swinging on a rope, holding a report card that read, "Calculus: A, Chemistry: A, Physics: A." His tagline was, "We Eliminate the Monkey Work of Memorization." If you've seen the modern classic film *Swingers*, you'll understand why I called him T$.

Drew came to the two-bedroom apartment that Edward "Teddy" Plaskon and I shared. Our pad was near the infamous UF Shands teaching hospital and close to campus. During high school at St. Jude's and St. Pete Catholic, I had never learned to factor in my math classes. I thought I understood exactly what the professors said, but I must have subconsciously resisted the curriculum's requirement to learn everything in the textbooks. I understood the first and second derivatives, the rates of change, but I just couldn't get my equations to add up there alone in a room with just me, pen, and paper. #Failure due to #indifference.

Drew made a valiant effort to get me a passing grade for the course. He patiently tried working with me to shift my focus away from parties, ladies, having fun, and other shiny objects. I signed up to give the course a second try and, not surprisingly, quickly found myself back in deep, cold waters. I think Drew learned a lot from me about partying, smoking, and "dealin" as the term was back then. I think if he hadn't been like *Rain Man* when it came to math (he scored perfectly on math in his SAT test), he'd have fallen into my party quicksand, too.

My inability to focus proved insurmountable for Drew and for me. Even with Drew's incredibly patient tutelage—and I mean incredibly patient—I couldn't sit still long enough to pass the finals in pre-calculus. I withdrew from UF before I did any real, permanent damage to my GPA. I think I was Drew's only tutoring failure. The bright spot was that Drew and I became blood brothers.

I had a tough decision to make in that summer of 1989. I couldn't figure out how I was going to break the news to my parents. "Hey, thanks for spending all this money on my classes, apartment, food, and utilities, but I'm so #selfish and #immature that I couldn't buckle down and pass this one class. Up until then, I got all A's and an occasional B in my other classes. It had been easy-peasy until now. There was nothing to do except pack up and drive the one hundred and fifty miles south, back to my childhood home.

The thought of moving back in with Mom and Dad is a kid's worst nightmare. It was back then, anyway. As I understand it, the kids don't want to leave home today. I have occasional stress-nightmares even today about being back at the university and not studying enough to pass my course. It's all very nebulous and vague—just the super-scramble (Drew's term) of "holy shit I forgot to study." These dreams are reminders of the humiliation I felt at the lowest of lows for me back in the summer of '89 (cue Bryan Adams). What seemed to be the worst summer of my life was about to get worse. Much worse.

I showed up at my parents' door with my tail between my legs and made the announcement that I was home from UF. It was pretty clear to them that the reason was that their son, "Michael Scott"—as Mom called me when she was *pissed*—had been in full party mode. Although I had been smart enough to leave before I did any permanent damage, I was, nevertheless, back home with my 'rents, completely humiliated.

I unpacked my stuff into my old bedroom, took a long, slow look around the room, and tried to compute the implications of how low I had sunk. I had no clue what I was going to do.

The first few days back home, I burned my car's tires around every corner – "drifting," as it's known today – and it dawned on me that my tires weren't going to last long. I had no money and no job. I had my usual endless energy, though, which I released by driving around town like a maniac, squealing tires on every corner. And I was still drinking around two six packs a day, plus those extras at party time.

It was a time in my life when I was struggling to get my act together. Kerry and Steve Mathieson owned John's Pass Liquors and Deli, where I worked off and on for the next three years. I learned a great deal about the hospitality industry: food prep, consistency in product, attention to customer service, cash management, and more. I was a good worker. I was reliable, and I learned the deli business while I was there. That meant slicing meats and cheeses, making deviled eggs, bacon, and Cuban sandwiches, toasting bread, the works. Consistency! I had many a burn on my forearms from the hot press we used to make Cubans. It was a full liquor store, and they carried over one hundred different beer labels in bottles and kegs. As a result, I learned to deal with unruly, drunken, and occasionally dangerous fishermen. Life there could be almost as dangerous as a bride who discovers that she has a broken zipper on her wedding dress just moments before her walk down the aisle.

As I look back at those days, I hope Kerry and Steve know how much I appreciate their support, mentoring, and patience at a difficult time in my life. They tolerated me when my talents were unchanneled and a little wild. If I were to paint a visual picture of myself at that point in my career, I would say, in most respects, especially outwardly, I was a wild, lady-chasing party boy who was into the hard-party lifestyle and drank way too much. My lifestyle was all about drinking, partying, volleyball, chasing the ladies, and smoking the good green herb now and again. I was attracted to lovely, bikini-clad ladies, who were always on the beach from every corner of the USA and beyond. They were literally everywhere, frolicking around, spending summers on our gorgeous, white sandy beaches.

I rationalized my unchanneled party-time, "dealin'" lifestyle by mis-defining it as a badge of honor, because that was how my peers and mentors measured success. My buddies and I used to try to identify what part of the country ladies were from by listening to their accents. Was Kristen from Ohio? Did Jenna come down from Michigan? I bet Jodie came down from Minnesota. Well, you get it. Fun times, for sure. Just not the right foundation for a successful life. I rationalized all of that by the old canard, "You are only young once." Just ask Oscar Wilde.

One morning, I was driving slow for a change and 100-percent sober. I lightly accelerated on a bit of road that was still wet from early-morning lawn sprinklers spraying into the street. I slowly accelerated just past the T.I. toll gate, literally one of the few times I was not monkeying around, #CrossMyHeart. With my dumbass bald tires, my baby Mustang GT—the pride and joy of a college guy's world—spun out of control just like my life. She took me into a 360-degree spin. The next second, I crashed her into the base of a street pole. My baby was totaled. The front, side, and hood were crushed. Ugh. Physically, I was fine, but everything else in my life was like my GT. A mess. And there was worse yet to come.

The summer of 1989 turned out to be a string of serial disasters waiting to happen. Besides dropping out of the University of Florida, the premier college in our state, and crashing my prized Mustang GT, I kept partying as if nothing had changed or needed changing. That, of course, was my problem. With my baby totaled, I had to ask Chris, my younger brother by five years, to use his scooter so I could have wheels. I thought I had fallen as far as I could go. My college boy identity—Michael with the inflated ego and self-styled Mister Cool with tinted windows and a fast dealin' car—was as crushed as my GT. When I looked at myself in the mirror, I saw Mister Cool riding a scooter to work. I couldn't stand that image of myself, so I talked with my good friend and bro, Michael Richards, into selling me exactly what I *didn't* need at that time.

I bought Richards's even faster and racier car, a white Pontiac Trans Am. It was a clone of the one that film star stud Burt Reynolds (RIP) made famous by eluding cops in his *Smokey and the Bandit* movies. Well, this one was all that Reynolds had and more. But, like the new owner, it had baggage. The AC was out, and it had a bothersome tranny problem. Transmission fluid constantly leaked onto the exhaust pipes. When idling at traffic lights in the brutal Florida summer heat and humidity, and with no AC, I inhaled noxious fumes that surrounded the car like mist from the Black Lagoon. It was a bad scene. #Humiliating. But I didn't care. It was fast, affordable, and it was mine.

While working at John's Pass Liquors and Deli, needless to say, I was drinking—always outside of work hours—like a fish. One or two after-shift drinks quickly turned into several more before rolling outbound. My station had me surrounded with an endless supply of those little airplane liquor bottles filled with all kinds of delightful spirits. To be clear, I only drank once while on the clock, and the owner, Steve, berated me for it. There was a pretty girl involved and yabba dabba do! I partied all the time except when working. I had a strong understanding of the discipline of separating work from play. Don't party during work. Ever. But after work, all bets are off.

One night, my coworker Ken and I were enjoying some loosening up time, talking shop, winding down after a long shift of dealing with the local drunken sailor stew. Ken is laser smart, and we enjoyed some deep, interesting conversations. Fifteen minutes easily turned into ninety minutes of shooting the shite. Before I knew it, I had busted two six packs of sixteen-ounce tall boys and a handful of those little mini bottles. So, I drove straight home and went to sleep, awoke early the next day, went for a 10K run, and had a raw egg shake before hitting the gym.

Not. What really happened next changed my life forever.

I did drive home to get freshened up, but it was for a late night. What could go wrong, right? I smoked a little herb and went out to do some more drinking. I don't recall much after that, but I know that two bars later, I was hammered. I raced my fast-as-fuck Trans AM down US 19. It was a car I took pride in because it could beat Mike Lewis' Corvette, and that pissed him off to no end.

This evening, barreling down US 19, drunk as fuck and imagining I was once again leaving Mike Lewis in my dust, and certainly heading to that next party, I heard the siren from Johnny Law as he pulled up behind me, flashing those terrifying red and blue lights. I was ripped. I pulled over, jumped out of my car, and staggered toward the officer with the declaration, "I'll straighten this out." Yeah, sure. The officer had other ideas.

One thing I do remember and will never, ever forget: Jail food sucks.

By the fall of 1989, I had my proverbial shit together. For the most part, I quit doing shots, as that always ended in chaos. I enrolled in St. Pete Junior College—ugh, again—to take a few more classes to get credits for my BS. I had to swallow my pride, returning from the elite U.F. back "down" to SPJC. And I was kick boxing at Amir's

In 1990, I decided I'd had enough BS. It was time to get serious about life and my future. I enrolled in USF and wrapped up my B.S. degree in Business Administration with a concentration in Marketing.

There is a strong correlation between high-level athletic training, like kickboxing, for example, and the amount of time you can/want to spend partying. You just cannot do both at the extreme and be good at either one. So, when I was kickboxing three, four, five, or sometimes six days a week, there was no room in my lungs for smokery. A few drinks, sure, but lungs filled with smoke on Friday night make you feel like you're underwater when you are inside the ring the next Tuesday. It's pipes out or lights out.

After getting my bachelor's degree, I was still in touch with my old circle of friends from the University of Florida. I kept in touch by phone with my good buddies and fellow Entrepreneurs, Teddy Plaskon, plus real estate guru Mike Lerner (RIP). They all moved up north after college and were freezing their asses off in the New Jersey winter.

I did a fair amount of trash talking on our calls, musing on how much I was enjoying my hot tub in Florida's warm January weather. I clinked the ice cubes in my cocktail glass so they were sure to hear them. I also shared how awkward I felt being distracted by several girls in the bar who were quite comfortable in their bikinis, while I was earnestly trying to carry on a phone conversation with them. In one of our calls, I casually mentioned that I had never experienced a real winter. I shared with them that I didn't know what snow and cold weather were like. My bestie, Teddy, dropped the dime and invited me up. I said, "Why not?" #LifeIsAnAdventure. Off to Clifton, New Jersey I went.

Ted's parents, Edward and Kathy Plaskon, were incredible. They welcomed me into their New Jersey digs with open arms. Ted's older brother Greg and his wife Geralyn were always kind to me. While I was there, I put in applications at Rutgers University and Montclair State University with the idea of continuing my postgraduate studies in business. In the meantime, however, I needed work, and I put some feelers out for a job.

A few days waiting for the phone to ring turned into several. I searched everywhere for some kind of decent work. *Ring. Ring, please!* I hoped. Finally, a call came from Teddy's pal, "Luche" Luciano. He said he'd found me a job if I could be there in thirty minutes. I about broke an ankle fumbling around in the utter blackness of Teddy's basement. After trying to change into work clothes, I thought, *WTF?* It was 5:00 AM, and I was hungover from a night of hardcore drinking. The room was spinning. "Dude, I'll be there in 30 minutes," I told Luche.

Fuck. It was like ten degrees outside. Me being a Florida native, I was ignorantly dressed as if I was going to the beach on a chilly Treasure Island afternoon. I didn't know it, but I was off to sell Christmas trees.

Ted's friend Luche introduced me my new boss, Dick Miller. It was freezing cold, and my job was simple: hang out all day and night in the harsh cold of a New Jersey winter selling six-foot, ten-foot, and fourteen-foot trees to very impatient and often rude Jersey residents. Dick gave me an old-school, rusty hand saw to use for cutting off the bottom two inches of the trees so they could absorb water in heated homes. #FreshCut. He didn't bother sharpening the saws from year to year, so cutting those trees was like cutting a steel pipe with a nail file. Each stroke found me wishing for at least a measly one-dollar tip. People usually stiffed me, especially those with their sweet $100K rides. The fir and pine trees oozed a sap that attached itself to everything I wore.

Fifteen minutes into my first dark morning—queasy and really, *really* hungover—I got a dressing down from the boss in front of everyone when I brought the customer a Douglas fir when she wanted another kind of tree, which in the freezing cold, 6 am haze of my hungoverness, all seemed the same to me. It was a dark winter morning in the midst of a nor'easter sleet-storm, and after literally less than half an hour on the job, Dick was threatening to demote me. I thought, demote me from what? *To* what? I'm a college grad with a business degree from a top school, and I am freezing my ass off working for him at five dollars an hour. #ABossWhoIsAptlyNamed.

Despite all of that, I had a great time, and, best of all, the Plaskons became family to me. If you're ever up there, schedule a stop at Fatsos (if it's still around), and, if you're brave, the Jersey Shore.

Ultimately, Florida beat out Jersey for my long-term plans, and I returned home to enroll back at USF to accumulate the remaining sixty credits needed for my MBA. I was so happy to be back in sunny St. Pete and Tampa, Florida.

I graduated from USF in 1993 with a master's degree in business with concentrations in economics and finance. I spent my first year working with one of the greatest legends in Florida real estate development, Charles Rutenberg. Charlie was a true grand master. I put my application onto a stack that had over two hundred other applicants. After making the first cut, I took a battery of tests, both intellectual and psychological. I surprised myself when I got the news that Rutenberg had selected me as his first choice. I did swing by the office several times during the process, being charmingly direct with my declarations that I "really, really, really" wanted this job. When I read my acceptance letter, I had further proof that, yes, I really could do whatever I put my mind to.

Working in the administration offices with Charlie enabled me to watch him scout and acquire raw land throughout Florida. I was part of his team involved in planning, design, and building entire neighborhoods. His operation sold homes by the thousands. We spent time on sites interacting with the carpenters and crews, at architects' offices, and in fabric and furniture stores. Then I spent months inside a model home, selling units. It was a complete home and neighborhood-building education. Charlie built much of the fabulous Countryside area and Ruth Eckerd Hall in Pinellas County. It was a priceless learning experience for anyone, especially a new college graduate who had a deep-rooted passion for real estate.

As Charlie announced his retirement, I began looking for a new job and left Rutenberg to go to work for a company called Western Photography (or something like that . . . I cannot recall their exact name). My buddy, Will Menyhurt, recommended me, knowing I needed fast cash and, being single, could zip around as I pleased.

My job description entailed traveling solo throughout the southeastern United States as an art and photography sales agent. I lived in roadside hotels and cooked my own (inexpensive) meals; it was adventurous in its own way. Most days, I set appointments calling on prospects that spread over ten to twelve hours. My commission rate was 18–24 percent, gross, so from out of that, I had to cover my own travel and living expenses. I covered Atlanta and Savannah in Georgia, then south to Lakeland, Miami, Tampa, Bonita Springs, and stops in between. Being on full commission, I strengthened my self-reliance, discipline, and tight budgeting, which were often not distinct in my past but became well proven on the road. The job had its downsides and could be a grind. No sales equaled no dinner.

Of all the places I visited during my year-long road tour around the southeast, a couple of cities stand out in my memory. Let me note that I believe odors picked up from our olfactory senses ingrain themselves into our memory. It's better to smell good ones with good vibes that evoke a pleasant atmosphere.

While working in Lakeland, Florida, one of my stops was located next to a bread factory. I scheduled meetings there that lasted all day. I recall the delightful aroma of Italian baked bread that I breathed in all day long (my ancestry is Novilla—thatsa nice). Another odor I recall emanated from a paper mill in a town somewhere in Georgia. It was so noxious that I didn't care at all about closing the deal. I just rushed through my presentation, desperate to escape. All I could think about was Mordor and Sauron and how to get as far away as possible.

A better memory from my salesman-on-the-road days was the time I spent with my pal from Boca Ciega High, Alex Brauch. Al and I knew the *Weird Science* film script by heart: "Greasy Pork Sandwich served in a dirty ashtray." Covering costs of traveling and being constantly on the road while depending on sales commissions had its dog days. Big Al and his lovely wife, Laurie, rescued me by opening their home to me while I was working in the Miami area. Such amazing humans—their kindness and patience have never been forgotten. It has come to my attention that good people, friendships, kindness, and remembering friends who were willing to help make up a recurring and highly positive theme.

After spending about a year on the road (think of Arthur Miller's play *Death of a Salesman*), I had saved some money, and, for some insane reason, I re-enrolled into USF, this time in their Psychology Master's and PhD program. A third of the way into my first semester, I had had enough. What was I thinking? I had zero education in all the medical terminology needed, and I was working as a traveling salesman spending sixty-plus hours a week on the road while trying to study and, of course, chase the ladies.

I had always had a strong desire to work for myself, and now seemed like the time to make that happen. Since working with Charles Rutenberg, I had nurtured the idea of creating my own real estate development company. After cutting the cord with USF and returning to my familiar stomping grounds, downtown St. Pete (DTSP), I set about establishing roots in real estate. As it turned out, those plans would be my business blueprint for several decades.

One of my first post-MBA adult decisions was to unburden myself from the daily overload of horrible news on TV and in the papers. When I was at college, I read the *St. Petersburg Times* (now the *Tampa Bay Times*) and *Wall Street Journal* first thing in the morning. Then I'd catch world and financial news on TV during the day and watch a final round of news in the evening just before bed. I wanted to stay current with what was happening in the world. But at some point, it became grossly apparent to me that news content was focused way too much on negative things in our world. It burdened my psyche. I wasn't comfortable being a passive consumer of all that news, and I was turned off by all their unceasing negativity. #CutTheCord.

Now that I was free from the responsibilities of my academic curriculum, I embraced my freedom to choose what really interested me rather than what news institutions told me I should be interested in. I said to myself, *Why go swimming through life with twenty-pound weights tied to my brain?* As far as I was concerned, the news was clickbait for businesses, disguised as objective sources of information. That is depressing. The business model of the news industry seemed mostly interested in attracting viewers in any way possible, and the formula used to accomplish this utilizes pain and misery. They are quite successful at it. These days, I don't have a newspaper subscription, and I avoid most spoon-fed TV news reports like the plague. Funny thing is, after freeing myself from negativity in the media, I feel like I have a healthier, more agile lifestyle.

I've always been a voracious reader, and one of my favorite books is *Think and Grow Rich* by Napoleon Hill. It was published in 1937 during the Great Depression era, and baby, he is (still) dead-on! The themes are mind over matter and mind over mind. Choose a career that empowers you to do what you love. When you work hard at it and stick with it, success follows. His book was a first of many self-help books and a precursor to classics like Tim Ferriss's *The 4-Hour Workweek*.

Being an Entrepreneur at heart—and always distracted by the next shiny object—I got an idea that was in the category of "stranger things could happen." I found an opportunity to jump into a comic book project called *Overworld*. It could have been epic. It was based on the incredible *Acts of Caine* series by the New York Times bestselling author Matthew Woodring Stover. Matt is a brilliant writer. His *Acts of Caine* series blended fantasy with sci-fi, and reading it was like drinking a perfect cup of cappuccino. It was genius storytelling. Readers—including me—were pissed off when we learned his series had ended. Like junkies, readers seemed to walk around in a daze, wanting more of his great stories.

Our team of Entrepreneurs included an old pal, Moe, along with his pal, Chris Jenkins. I helped fund and assemble a talented team of artists and original thinkers, and we started out with high hopes. Think *Game of Thrones*. Yeah. It could have reached that level of goodness. Alas, what we all ended up with instead was a Red Wedding. Nevertheless, I am grateful that Matt and I remain friends. #HardKnocks. It was a high-risk project and another difficult learning opportunity for a guy I know well, Michael Scott Novilla.

One of the primary lessons I gained from that experience was this: When a project has substantial risk, and you're funding it, control the money flows and be a primary decision-maker. The experience did test my belief that failure is a great teacher and always offers learning moments—if you are open to changing and improving yourself. One good thing about this failure was meeting Chris Jenkins, a webmaster, tech guru, and human extraordinaire who has proven to be worth every penny I lost in the *Overworld* project. I always joke that I got Chris and his superstar wife, Kym, "in the divorce."

Speaking of improving, it's something I love to do. When I visit a home, store, or restaurant, I find myself studying the lighting or the furniture arrangement, mentally designing ways to improve them. I literally can't stop myself. Recently, I was in a restaurant waiting to order a meal and noticed that the font on their menu was far too small to read easily. I asked to talk to the manager, and I shared my

> editorial thoughts with her. Sharing your ideas—even about menu fonts—is a small way to add value for others. It's a model anyone can use to help make our world a better place. I constantly tell hotel managers to add labels to their breakfast buffet offerings. Soy sauce isn't Balsamic vinegar. Or is it? If one person is better off, everyone wins. #WinWin.

My post-graduate experience working alongside Charlie Rutenberg nurtured an even deeper love for real estate. As a kid, I loved building things and studying design. In the late 80s, I got my Florida Real Estate license, then my broker's license. I started out with the venerable Century 21, then spent five years with Prudential, and finally worked with the ERA brand. All the while, I thought about strategies to identify areas in St. Petersburg that were poised for growth. St. Pete at that time was at the pre-start-up phase, so to speak, just beginning to start to develop into the dynamic city it is now. It seemed blatantly obvious to me that static neighborhoods from the old era were going to be filled in with new homes and businesses that brought new energy. Strategically, it was a no-brainer.

I developed a business model to begin purchasing, renovating, and leasing single and multi-family homes. I focused on small (two to twelve-unit) apartments situated in a beautiful area of fifty-six acres at the heart of the city's downtown called Crescent Lake. It was a slice of pure heaven that was teeming with Florida's beautiful landscapes and wildlife.

I also considered properties in the core downtown area that were burdened by something of a skid row identity.

Transiting through DTSP then was like leafing through the pages of a dark, comedic, zombie comic book. There were run-down buildings populated by filthy street denizens, a myriad of aggressive prostitutes, and its share of the mentally ill and homeless.

I made my first investment in 1995 in an eight-unit, two-building apartment at 326 6th Avenue North. This address was ground zero of the DTSP zombie community. What made it strategic was that it was only blocks away from what is now the 5-Star Vinoy Renaissance Hotel. I was a confident, twenty-seven-year-old Entrepreneur—college-educated, born and raised in the same city as the property I wanted to purchase. All I needed was funding, and I was confident that I could get a loan. Oh, how naive I was to think that bankers thought like me, through the proactive lens of a forward-thinking Entrepreneur. Sigh.

The ROI (return on investment) looked good. My attorney and pharmacist father was a respected, active member of our community. I myself had a Florida real estate broker's license and a solid record of success for over five years. I had an MBA, and the property was available at a price that represented the bottom of the current real estate market cycle. My contract to purchase was $80K for an eight-unit property, located within sight of the downtown waterfront. It was a slam dunk. . . . Not.

The bank's loan committee apparently viewed me through a lens of "insufficient liquidity/collateral" and "lack of experience." They rejected my income property loan application. WTF? They would have written a check to me for a car loan in the same amount and sat back in their cushy boardroom chairs as they watched me drive off the lot and into depreciation alley. My FICO scores were healthy. The investment was certain to contribute to the renaissance of DTSP. I argued my case for the application, and they laughed. I was just too early and didn't have that sexy balance sheet that bankers love to drool over. The saying goes that bankers love to loan you money when you don't need it. Today, the value of that property exceeds my most optimistic expectations back then. #Spineless. #WithoutVision.

Steve and Kerry, my old friends, offered me much-needed guidance as I navigated the world of real estate financing. I pitched them, and, after agreeing to the terms, we created a partnership to manage the purchase, renovation, leasing, and managing of this same 326 6th Avenue North property. Those eight units needed a complete makeover. They were a major mess. Smoke had stained everything, and the carpets had been soaked and soiled since before the Harry S. Truman administration. The rooms had literally seventy years' worth of nicotine, bodily fluids, and stench baked in. Disgusting. Our first tenant was a young man who thought he was a vampire. I kid you not. He even acted and dressed like one.

Over a period of several years, our team shared laughs, calluses, and plenty of tears on our first project. The partnership and support we had was an important turning point in my life. I continued down the road that took me away from a hard-partying lifestyle and toward the much brighter, 24/7/365 lifestyle of an investment property owner. On that road, I learned to deal with fellow human beings in a much healthier and more positive way. There were challenges and many disgusting occasions, like the time I discovered that a tenant had flushed his underwear down the toilet. The endless backed-ups, overflowing sewers—oh my, what a shite show! (By the way, check out my just-for-fun restroom review website Shite.Show.)

Here are the gory facts. On a Super Bowl Sunday, I had my friends over to watch the game. A rare few hours to relax. We were settling in for the kickoff when my phone rang. My tenant advised me, "Uh, Mike, my toilet is backed up and overflowing everywhere. Get right over here, man." Fuck. Life as a landlord is a bitch. Off I dutifully went, leaving my guests to fend for themselves in my living room. I grabbed my trusty, rusty Roto-Rooter snake, two kinds of plungers, a pair of long-ass rubber gloves, and a pair of shit shoes because it was gonna be messy.

As a landlord, I got to be the neighborhood expert on shit. I was able to watch solids, loosies, corn chunks, diarrhea, toilet paper, tampons, kid's toys, condoms, (used and new, unopened packs), and everything you can imagine and much you can't imagine that went floating past the clean-out of my apartment units. You see, the plumbing into your home or apartment unit runs fresh water into it. Then, after being used at your sink and toilet, the gray (dirty) water is sent through pipes and ultimately into the main sewer lines. From there, it goes into the city's water treatment plant.

Well, this time, I simply couldn't unclog this tenant's toilet drain. The two gents living there swore by everything holy that they had never put anything down there to cause such a horrible backup. (Do you know the level of lies told to landlords? I do, and they are endless.)

At this point, I am imagining the Super Bowl party going on in my living room without me while I am trying not to kill anyone. An hour or so passes, and, after getting soaking wet in shit water, I called Jon "Jonny" Aljasir, my brother from another mother and master plumber pal.

Jonny used his industrial-rated snake to hook a pair of the tenant's underwear.

It turns out, my tenant had a "friend" over, and, unbeknownst to his live-in partner, problems arose that required a pair of underwear to be flushed to hide evidence. OMG. I don't give a rat's ass about who my tenants are kissing or banging, but please, ladies, gents, and questioning detectives, don't ever flush your underwear down anyone's toilet. Never fucking *ever*! Especially my toilet on Super Bowl Sunday.

This is way too much information, I know. But knowing that I could literally call (bull)shit on this stew of lies, I discreetly peeked into my tenant's dresser drawers the following day to solve this mystery. Not surprisingly, the pair fished from the toilet matched the tenant's preferences (in drawers), and was confirmed in his drawers. They were red nut-huggers. I'll never ever forget them. The offending garment was the same brand and size that my tenant kept right there in his drawer. Takeaway: Tenants lie like partner-cheating brother-fuckers. Ugh!

My hyperactive, inquisitive, go-at-them personality—which, in my youth, had been a burden—resolved itself into a great resource as a grown adult. I continued to acquire focus, as well as the desire to move in a more creative, positive direction. I tried writing (on the side) for a while and wrote a comedic screenplay entitled *Landlord*, which was taken from my experiences—wait for it—as a landlord. Duh. It's sitting on "the shelf," unpublished, although I go back and read it now and then, which typically provokes a gut-busting episode of laughter. It is a juvenile narrative, but humorous, nonetheless. (I included a red underwear murder scene. OMG!)

My co-writer is a friend of mine, my fratello (brother) Michael E. Graf. Mike is a highly talented comedic writer and a hilarious guy in person. The story was kind of prescient in one sense because it anticipates today's cable news dominated the world. It features a news organization called BNN: Bad News Network. Its business model is to saturate news consumers (us) with a steady stream of negative news. All negativity, all the time. In our story, the landlord has a fair share of dark humor, lots of crackhead jokes, and crazy headlines reported by the BNN anchor. One BNN headline read, "Toddler drowns in milk as the world runs out of cheese." I mean, how ridiculous is that? I wrote this script to release my pent-up frustration about the institutional media and as the lie-absorbing landlord.

Part of my frustration came from living life as a 24/7/365 landlord, dealing with lying, stealing, dirty, nasty, untrained, and mostly noisy motherfucking tenants. It took a toll on me. Our building was in a rough area, attractive to and surrounded by low-grade humans. One tenant drank and behaved like Jim Morrison but without Jim's charm or voice. He liked to slam doors and scream at his filthy, streetwalking, live-in girlfriend. He was so loud that the other tenants couldn't ignore him. I accepted him as my tenant, thinking, "Where do these people come from?"

I couldn't possibly make this shit up. And long-term landlords out there know exactly what I'm saying. Being a hands-on landlord, living in the same building with my tenants—all of us at the bottom tier of the food chain, so to speak—made me wonder daily how we have survived this long as a species. (Shudder.)

Nevertheless, I put my head down and kept my real estate investment footprint expanding. I focused on acquiring every building I could in the Crescent Lake neighborhood. I acquired vintage (meaning run-down) buildings, typically built in the 1920s through the 1960s. I assembled an incredibly talented crew, including Deb Siegel, Jakub Kulakowski, painter Keith 'Hippie' O'Loughlin, the Aljasir brothers, roofer Jeff Flynn, and our godfather, Michael 'Mikey' Ruggieri. We became family, and I'm honored to my core for our continued friendship. Then, after about seven years of 24/7 managing, renovating, leasing, and land-lording, I took some much-needed and well-deserved time off. It was early in the new millennium, and I had an itch to travel the world. Put more directly, I needed to get the hell outta DTSP.

I decided to visit Europe to take in the world's great art galleries and swankiest of lounges. I was researching a concept: art gallery meets lounge meets event space. I began imagining a new kind of business model that combined all three, anchored by art. Conceptually, I wanted an art gallery (sexy, fun, unique, inviting, and thought-provoking) in a swanky lounge environment. I imagined a place where James Bond felt right at home. My vision was for a business model that centered around a lounge environment with a hip, cool, dark, alluring, and, most of all, fun experience. Oh, and by the way, the landscape had to serve as a 5-Star event space. I began thinking about an open, flexible floor plan to accommodate this concept.

After returning home to St. Pete, I scouted potential renovation sites that could serve as a home for this ambitious goal. I looked at one building that was run as a full-on funeral home. Another had once been a church. I wanted a property that spoke to me. My evaluation process combined the tangibles such as square feet, location, price, parking, etc, with the intangibles, such as an environment that communicated positive vibes and evoked the gut feeling of a great gathering place.

I did walkthroughs and examined each structure's bones and history. My search took me all of 2004 and 2005. I finally found a vintage building on 9th Street North, a street which was later renamed in honor of Dr. Martin Luther King Junior. My art lounge concept found its home at 535 Dr. M. L. King Junior Street North. Hence, I use the address in my brand, NOVA 535. "Nova" means new, and "supernova" communicates the idea of a new universe. (The history of the 535 building is something of a furry tale—more about that later.)

I assembled a team of contractors to begin renovating the building and was lucky enough to work with some incredibly talented people. I laid out a renovation plan for our team to work from as we began this challenging new project together.

I have to say, it's hard to make money in the art world. Entering a landscape that sells fine art is a PITA (pain in the ass). An art gallery's space tends to be the playground of the rich. I researched several mid-sized event venues that were successful, and I found they had creative, hard-working business leadership at the top who had found innovative ways to survive their tough first years. Most importantly, these art Entrepreneurs focused on team roles and systems in an effort that demanded continuous improvement.

I looked for guidance from my business consultant, ole T$, Drew Edwards. My revenue projection from the art sales side of the business came out to be, at most, 1 percent of the total revenue, and I quickly decided that the art component's value was not as a revenue producer but more as a sexy and unique backdrop that could be a platform for the real business: a 5-Star lounge and event venue.

I had to take a realistic view of my own personal history. As a younger man, the event I had run was dubbed the "Beach Life Party Man Competition," competing at the all-pro level. Now, I was forty years old, and the hard-partying lifestyle I had lived throughout my teens, twenties, and thirties was fading into the past. I was 100 percent certain that I could not create a business model that had me involved in a traditional bar, late night after night after night. I knew all too well the schedule and the baggage attached to that kind of future. I didn't see myself closing at two or three in the morning, followed by two hours of cleanup and the obligatory EON (end of night) closing procedures. Also, there are the inevitable after-shift drinks and occasional smokery. That model would see me doing last call somewhere around 4:30, 4:45, or, shit, 5:00 AM, thinking ironically to myself, *It's 5 AM Go Home!* I imagined that on some nights, I would find myself someplace along Dale Mabry for a nightcap, trying to unwind from the previous night's event. I envisioned barely getting to sleep by sunup or maybe catching a third wind and thinking, *It's 5 AM What's Next?*

Thinking about all that, I told myself, "No way, Mike. Stay focused." I mean, Mons Venus is open until six AM most days, and I know the wild n' crazy stuff going on there peaks from two to six—thank you, Joe Redner! In case you don't know, Joe invented the nude lap dance. I was fortunate enough to talk with Joe several times; he reminds me of Stan Lee (RIP). They are both visionaries, doing exactly what they love for a living, and doing it well. Along the way, they pushed the boundaries. Joe's business model is great, but running a bar means being up until four AM, five AM, or six AM almost every night of the week. That train has left the station for me. My future is in the live event business.

I made the decision not to go backward. The NOVA Way is forward progress and continuous improvement.

I got my first job when I was eleven, and since then, there was only one when summer I didn't work. True enough, I liked to party, but when I wasn't partying, I worked extremely hard. I turned a corner in my forties and made a solid commitment that my top priority was to take this concept of an art lounge meets swanky event space and make it into a solid success. My team was going to do it right from day one. I was always eco-friendly and LGBTQ-plus friendly (there may be more letters by the time this gets into print). The business model is profitability *and* sustainability. We were thinking lean, green, and clean. We love every color in the rainbow. Our target was to get as close to perfect as possible. That is the NOVA Way.

I looked for a simple theme that our team could remember as we moved forward through the decision-making processes for the development of the NOVA Way. I came up with the phrase "world-class and sexy." That is our team's standard. Anything that doesn't fit the world-class and sexy model is going to be excluded from our plans.

World-class and sexy is a filter designed to capture value and let everything else go. Ask anyone on our team, and they know that. I remind them every day, "Guys, it has to be world-class *and* sexy." They have heard it so often that they've started finishing my sentences. It has become part of our value-added model, and we use it often as our black/white, pass/fail test.

The idea is all about creating a timeless experience for our guests. We intentionally exclude the trendy and fashionable-at-the-moment motif. In fact, the finished space has no carpeting. I found and installed beautiful, durable (and expensive) Brazilian hardwood floors and, after removing two to three inches of plaster, cleaned and restored the original 1920s rare red clay tile walls. Next,

I added ribbed glass windows and doors, plus utilized other classic materials like granite and wrought iron.

Visit NOVA 535 today to experience our timeless motif. The design philosophy is borrowed from the black tuxedo that debuted more than a century ago and endures as a style-setter to this day. It evokes a James Bond look. Sexy, powerful, and timeless, just like a martini—shaken, not stirred. That is the driving force behind the NOVA Way: timeless, world-class, and sexy.

I have been blessed to have made so many cool, hip, edgy friends with impulses to create cutting-edge ideas years ahead of their time. We have a team of influencers, trendsetters, and social stallions. I surf in the wake of their cutting-edge coolness, which helps make me think I am cool also. I benefit by association.

I will share a secret to success: Surround yourself with people who are smarter than you and who compete amongst each other with their fresh, innovative ideas. Our brand is forward-thinking, always ahead of the curve. My Entrepreneurial family makes me work to keep up since they are constantly pushing the envelope. I agree with that well-known TED-talker who said you are the average of the five people you spend most of your time with; words of wisdom.

I gave a lot of thought to my role as a team leader. I want my management style to provide clarity for everyone so that they know, yes, Michael is the boss and signs the checks. (Well, actually, everything is digital these days, because we went paperless years ago with the help of our bookkeeper extraordinaire, Krystle Pinzker. Thanks, KP.)

My own memories as an employee often remind me that the boss isn't always right. Now that I'm the leader of a major investment development, that fact is important to keep in mind. My team understands that I expect them to contribute and nurture the NOVA vision. That means that they have to create from strong, unique points of view. Our modus operandi is to battle our ideas out in the arena of the real world.

My 5-Star wedding and event venue would never have become the success it is with a spineless team of, "Yessir, Mr. Michael, sir." Our routine is all about the give and take through an exchange of different ideas. That often involves arguments and occasional verbal fights. We occasionally are literally yelling and screaming at one another, but ultimately, we sort out the average, and the not good enough, in favor of only the best for NOVA. That synergy gives a spark to our organization.

As Emily Morgavan, our amazing designer, says of NOVA 535, "This baby had a difficult birth." Emily is so right, and she helped to nurture NOVA 535 out of a "man cave" environment into a harmonious, yin-yang, balanced, world-class event space. She and I sometimes fight for days over the best designs for NOVA. We are a perfect design duo, each strong and committed.

Emily and I worked on the signature design and architecture for the twin staircases inside our main gallery at NOVA 535. We were desperate to find that perfect solution. Emily wanted them to embrace guests like welcoming arms, inviting our patrons to discover the mysterious second-floor landscape. We engaged a steel artist named Michael Aaron. Imagine a classic late-1800s boxer—good looking, with the handlebar mustache, built like a brick shit house—and you'll see what Michael Aaron looks like. Nicest guy you could imagine. He's a world-class and sexy wrought iron god. He saved us. Emily and I drew out our crazy concept, and yup, he built it. Today, our twin staircases greet guests in the downstairs gallery like a big smile. They are so sexy and spectacular.

NOVA would have been a stillbirth without Emily's midwifery. I'm eternally grateful for her. If you're ever lucky enough to meet Emily, beg her to show you her crazy lady face sketches. They, like Emily, are uniquely amazing!

During the long process of building out NOVA 535, I was rescued innumerable times by amazing people, like Jennifer Silva, who also became close friends of mine. We met on an American Stage trip to Toronto, Ontario. My parents made reservations for themselves to go on the two-week excursion, and my mom decided she had to stay home. I picked up her ticket, and because Jen and I were the youngest on the tour—by at least two decades—we became great friends. From Jennifer came Michael Aaron. Love them both dearly!

Funny enough, on that precious trip with my father Michael Francis Novilla (RIP) and Jennifer, we were in Toronto for the opening night of *Mamma Mia*, which was July 22, 2001. Just about 20 years later, that show is still being shown and enjoyed by audiences across the globe. Timeless is our enjoyment of and struggles with complicated love stories and family dramas. Strangely enough, it's playing here in St. Pete as I write this, performed by our fantastic local American Stage in the Park, where I've seen dozens of incredible shows. Wow! Full circle!

Chapter 4

Building NOVA 535

Negotiations to purchase our NOVA 535 building lasted more than a year. The investment took all my savings: $500,000. Literally every nickel I had. I borrowed the rest from Mike Lewis and (eventually) Mike Mitchell and took ownership in late 2005.

The building had an original use going way back to 1920 as a five-and-dime store called Slap Happy's. I mentioned earlier that the backstory of this venue is something of "a furry tale." When I bought the building, it was being run as a doggie daycare and pet kennel called Pet Planet. I told my friends, "Don't be surprised when you see it, because it's really in 'ruff' shape." When the team saw it the first time, their jaws dropped. They couldn't believe I was serious. I had some major convincing to do to win them over. It was, to put it bluntly, in terrible, terrible condition. The front exterior facade was the only decent feature I could point to.

When it was still in operation, Pet Planet had three sections, west to east. Entry through the front door from M.L.K. Street led into a large room about twenty feet deep. This was Pet Planet's retail sales space. They sold pet food, leashes, pet toys, etc., and they had their cash register there to collect for grooming and boarding. This was by far the nicest interior section of their building. The beautiful red clay was exposed like a taut, stretched bikini, hinting at the beauty that lay behind her large plaster cracks. (For great before and after photos, check out Its5amGoHome.com.)

When I looked up, I could see all the way to the original finished sixteen-foot ceilings. This entry retail area encouraged me, and I grew more confident in the building's potential. That gave me the courage and fortitude for what came next.

I navigated deeper into the bowels of the dark building, accompanied by the stench of piss and shite, and the shrill barking from more dogs than I could count, as my first nightmare began. I exited the retail area through a lime green colored door. I'll never forget that color. I felt like I was like entering a different building with its own alternative universe. I thought out loud, "What the *fuck* have I gotten myself into?"

Pet Planet had an indoor kennel functioning within the building's footprint. A chain link fence carved up the main room. The ceiling had shrunk from its grandiose sixteen-foot height down to eight feet. The beautiful clay brick walls were covered in thick plaster. The sights and sounds from a full-on kennel experience were overwhelming. Then suddenly, there they were: the little doggie residents happily shitting, pissing, scratching, and, most annoying of all, barking incessantly. It was sensory overload!! Stop, please!

Years before, I remember taking my two super cute toy poodles, Maxwell and Malcolm, into Pet Planet along with my (still) good friend and now ex-girlfriend, Melissa Caban. She is an incredibly talented graphic designer and a lovely human being. Melissa invested the first two years of our relationship into getting me to agree to have a toy poodle, the kind she had enjoyed when she was a little girl. I'm a huge dog lover, and Melissa is smart, beautiful, persistent, and makes perfect arguments. She convinced me that toy poodles don't shed, and are highly intelligent and cute. She also mentioned a couple of times that they are small and super-easy to manage. Small dogs mean small poops. Eventually, of course, she got the toy poodles.

I continued my safari deeper and deeper into the abyss, focused on finding the east side of the building as a destination. Here, I discovered the third and final ground floor section, which was a dedicated space for pet grooming. It was layered with a thick accumulation of doggie hairs, toenails, furballs, odd-colored stains, puddles of various sizes and consistencies—and did I mention their shit was splattered everywhere? The word "disgusting" doesn't do memories of the scene justice!

In retrospect, it was fortunate for NOVA and her thousands upon thousands of delighted future guests that I didn't abandon my instinct and vision right then and there. If I had followed a detailed budget with a business plan and those other things that the suits of this world insist on, I would have made an about-face and walked out long before risking my $500K along with Mike and Mike's money.

I spent two years (sixty credits) getting my MBA from USF (go Bulls!), and I knew what was involved in creating a business plan. It means months of research, spreadsheets, charts, and forecasts, with much of the data ultimately being useless, because no one can accurately predict much about the future. An investor with "suits" for advisors would have made his way out the door, into a BMW, and off to a more conventional investment property, posthaste.

Sometimes, a person has to take chances with nothing but his dreams and huevos. Intuitively, I felt the magic of this building. The old girl and I had lots of positive (pet) energy, and she gave me good vibes. It was like Gandalf the Gray, in serious need of a magical bath. Ultimately, our girl got a three-year-long deep soaking and scrubbing at an ultimate cost of just about $3,000,000.

After we did the post-purchase walkthrough of the 535 building, and after the two Mikes' monies and my own life savings were committed, I thought to myself, *Holy shit, Michael, what did you get yourself into?*

Alas, the old girl was suffering from decades of serious neglect and abuse, but I saw she had hidden and redeeming qualities: Her bones were good, and her walls were gorgeous. There was enough quality there to pique my excitement. I was smitten by her rare red clay tile block walls and classic brick columns over steel beams. Unfortunately, at that time, these features were mostly obscured by several inches of plaster layered all over the top of her. I found an old-style lathe and plaster ceiling sixteen feet above her badly cracked terrazzo floor. It was impossible to determine what the "finished" ceiling height was, at first, since it was covered at its eight-foot level by a false drop-ceiling made up of the ugliest gray panels imaginable. It had the worst of 1980s style written all over it. Visually, the ceiling panels were mostly stained and broken, and in terms of the olfactory experience, they smelled beyond terrible.

There was literally dog shit and piss all over the floor. Our team found hairs of every kind and description from every breed of dog and cat imaginable. It was impossible to inspect or work in that environment without face masks—which, in fact, we wore for the first few years. It was filth at a level of disgust that would make a billy goat puke and even tough-as-nails Rambo gag. Sucio!

There were more surprises. I found a second hidden drop-ceiling hung with a grid made from steel wires at a height of twelve feet above the floor. The environment reminded me of a depressing call center or perhaps a DMV (department of motor vehicles) building. It visually assaulted visitors as soon as they entered. It was the perfect fit for a scene from the *Landlord* script Mike Graf and I had written. Better yet, it would be the perfect Bad News Network HQ.

The funny thing was that, in those days, the buildings did not skimp on materials. They used real steel, plenty of concrete, and real thick-ass clay-fired bricks. The sections of that drop ceiling were supported with steel that couldn't be cut with a Sawzall. We had to detach them by hand, one-by-one, while balancing on a forklift. It was long, aggravating, arduous, and physically draining work. But we kept at it, and eventually, ciao bella!

Our plans called for 50 percent of the building's space to be dedicated for NOVA 535's main gallery, and because that space was hidden by those two drop ceilings, I had to literally work blind during the initial planning and design phase. Fortunately, I love demo work, and the uncertainty attached to it was like an adventure for me. When I'm into busting walls and tearing down ceilings, I get inspired. It's as if I'm on an Indiana Jones hunt for treasure, looking for the Lost Ark. It helps to be an optimist when you are invested in a repurposing and renovation project with substantial financial risk.

This project called up memories of time I spent with my incredible father, Michael F. Novilla, when I traipsed alongside him as he inspected his clients' homes and condos. He was a probate, wills, and trust attorney, so he had to certify the property and estates for clients (post mortem) when there were no family members residing locally. Dad would have to go to their homes, identify important documents, things of value, etc. I enjoyed tagging along, and I loved to let my imagination soar every time one of the creaky old doors in these dark, vacant homes swung open. We discovered lifetimes of memories and possessions. "Look and don't touch" was Dad's mantra. Seeing his clients' photos, their antiques, and lifetime collections was an experience that made me feel like I had my own personal internet of things (IOT) in a kid's imaginary universe. As I began tearing down NOVA's false walls and drop ceilings, I found myself transported back by those childhood memories of my old neighborhood and time spent with Dad. #Exploring.

Her two suspended ceilings took a lot of time to remove. It was slow, painstaking, hot, sweaty, and nasty, dirty work. Then we spent six months taking out interior walls, plus all the old plumbing, wiring, and the original 1920s lathe and plaster ceiling. I swear, I heard the old girl let out a huge sigh of relief as we unburdened her from the decades of useless weight she'd had to carry for all those years. The lathe and plaster alone easily weighed a ton. In my imagination, I thought I could hear her whisper softly, "Thank you, Michael," as she shed all those unnecessary pounds.

With her old onerous infrastructure gone, we discovered a beautiful blank canvas we could work from as we dove into the creative phase of our journey of discovery to unlock the hidden treasures inside NOVA 535. Mike Lewis was my initial private banker. (There should be a song parody of the song "Private Dancer." "He's my Private Banker, he does it for money.") Mike and I were childhood friends who morphed into partners in real estate financing together in the 1990s, and, as Mr. Lewis loves to say, "Here we grow again." He liked to swing by and watch our renovation progress to share his input and expertise. We liked it when Mike was accompanied by his beautiful, smart, and super sweet wife, Samantha. Sammy always brought value-added with her. The Lewis family has big money, so these days, Mike spends more of his time on the golf course and playing with his three beautiful kids, Max, Mitch, and Marin, and not so much time sweating it out with us regular, 99 percent people in old, filthy buildings.

My other partner, Mike Mitchell, on the other hand, is a true hands-on guy. He was all over the battle zone, down into the trenches and up on the roof—whatever it took. His decades of serious construction knowledge proved invaluable. And just when the Great Recession hit us, Mike came to the rescue with a cash infusion that was life-saving. That happened when the motherfucking banks morphed into fair-weather friends and withdrew their real estate lending and all other available credit. Mitchell quite literally saved the day. Mike Mitchell knows my gratitude is bottomless, but for the written record, right here, thank you, Mike Mitchell!

If there weren't lenders like Mike and Mike, who took the risk ride along with us visionaries, then the entire world would look like boring strip malls. No design aesthetics, no world-class and sexy. Instead, it would all focus solely on "profit maximization." It takes the disciplined investor to save the money, which is a difficult skill to maintain over the long run. Money is so easy to spend and lose, so hard to maintain and grow. Thank you again, Mike and Mike.

The Great Recession was a double-whammy for businesses. I survived three recessions prior to that one because there was always credit and money available. In good times, I had to pay 3 percent interest and zero points. Choppy waters, and maybe it went as high as 9 percent interest and one point. During the serious recession with historic high interest rates, I had to pay 18–21 percent with five to ten points. The thing is, there were always "hard money" lenders around. They were expensive, true, but they were reliable, nonetheless. The Great Recession was the first time in my professional life that I lost access to all available cash and credit resources. The banks pulled the personal credit on every one of my credit cards and credit lines. I can't stop thinking about those "spineless mother-fuckers," even decades later. Why? I had a perfect credit record for over twenty years. I paid my loans on time and did everything by the book. #Betrayal.

I had to scramble to sell all my properties. It was like losing a twenty-year-old child in a car accident or from a sudden illness. Twenty years of sweat, tears, bloodshed, nightmares, hard work, and stress. Poof. Bye-bye. Vanished. The evil "black swan" came knocking at my door and demanded an offering. It was either my 100 Crescent Lake apartments (the mom) or my new baby, NOVA 535. It was a terrible, humbling, and awful experience. I felt like I'd been hit in the face. I recalled my experience at Boca Ciega high, when I was walking around campus with a big fat black eye. Then I recalled Amir's voice—his imploring and his screams. "Mike, get your hands up and fight."

The banks pulling my credit left a terrible taste in my mouth and made me realize how quickly things could be lost. Poof! I suffered through foreclosure on one of my single-family investment properties. I didn't react fast enough, and I resisted the idea of filing for bankruptcy. I was like a eunuch. Or maybe like the walking dead. (I still haven't watched that show, by the way.)

My world today is different. My business model is all about organic client growth and staying debt-free. I don't owe any money except for my original real estate loans from buddies, Mike (Lewis) and Mike (Mitchell). It feels great to be financially independent and be able to say, "fuck you" to the banks. Cyber currencies are coming, and I can see an end to the reign of those fair-weather bankers thanks to the new digital landscape. I am thinking about encrypted mobile digital payments. Ah, yes. . . . But that's another tale for another day.

To be clear, the banks can be—and are—extremely useful. My experience, however, has taught me to understand that your relationship with them can be quickly and arbitrarily terminated at their soul(less) discretion, and you and your business can be left dead as a doornail. It's better if your business creates its own sustainable financial power organically, which places you in much better control of your future.

It wasn't until I read *The Black Swan* by Nassim Taleb, that I fully grasped the whole black swan theory—the idea that an event can be unable to be predicted in advance yet seem inevitable in hindsight. By then, I had learned the hard way what the lenders were doing to everyone, including me, during those times. If you had a LOC (line of credit) backed by an asset (building) or you had a written, personal credit guarantee for, say, $100,000, and your cash advance was $35,000, that left you with a $65,000 line of available credit. That was the kind of credit I depended on for renovations and to buy goods and services, etc. Well, during the banking crisis in 2008, the banks dropped their credit lines to whatever amount you already owed, so your $65,000 (of no longer available credit) was literally gone without warning.

The banks took away hundreds of thousands of dollars of available credit from me in a matter of weeks. Try sleeping when all your finances dry up and you've got only a few months and a bunch of expenses left to go until project completion. What a nightmare!

Repeating Myself: This was not the loss of future monies promised, like, "Hey, we decided not to give you that loan, sorry." That also happened. This was the *existing* lines of credit (equity lines, credit cards, etc.) which the banks wiped out. They deleted all the existing available credit. Poof. Bye-bye. Time to cry.

Fortunately, the demolition of the building's interior gave me an outlet to vent my frustrations and also added fun to our otherwise long, dirty, and grueling work days. There were other lessons to be learned. It's easier to tear something down than build it up.

Construction is like a war. You will find landmines everywhere. Contractors will screw you up one side and down the other, and costly mistakes will happen. It's not a matter of if, but when. Ask me about the guy who cut through our main gallery's electrical wiring, with about forty branches, literally *moments* after I told him to avoid all the wires. I pointed out exactly what to cut and what not to cut. Seconds later, *fuck*! On that occasion, $3,000 and a week's worth of work went *poof* with a squeeze of a Sawzall's trigger. Renovation and construction is a rough, dirty war, fought daily. Like real war, you better be vigilant every second of every damn day.

It's best to follow along behind your contractors and clean up after them, always prepared to fill in the gaps and the missing pieces. I tried to not get frustrated, and I supported my contractors by being on-site each and every day from sunrise to well past sunset. The general needs to be on the battlefield, and that is exactly where I was. If you're ever lucky enough to meet him, buy Mike Mitchell some lunch and ask him about contractors and costly mistakes. It'll be one long, enlightening dining experience.

Friends often stopped by to watch the work progress, and many responded by referring their friends (who were strangers to me) to help out. They brought expertise great and small to the table and helped with the difficult work of creative planning and design. I asked them a million questions. My vision for a sexy, world-class art lounge/event space came from a core belief that drove the buildout for our artsy 535 building. Creating is often about having a clear vision, a commitment to continuous improvement, and a "good is never good enough" attitude. Strategic planning helps, although I'm more about getting things rolling and making plans along the way, for better or worse.

My vision for opening an art gallery + swanky lounge + event space = art lounge was finally steaming full-speed ahead. As we progressed through the buildout, I eventually realized we couldn't just order materials and start banging away with hammers. Our team had to engage in nonstop brainstorming and creative meetings each day. We made drawings on the backs of napkins and both sides of envelopes, and we even did pencil drawings on walls with cryptic notes below. Whatever idea anyone had, we followed a team model that was heavy into communication and sharing. We learned to borrow from each other's inspiration, and, in the process, we created a strong bond.

Where's the right spot for the bar? Our kitchen? The restrooms? Everyone contributed. Someone seemed to rise up at their best moment to channel the team's energy and inspiration back in the right direction.

At this time, Jim Walker, our electrician and eventually part of my family, joined the group. I called Jim "the Pirate" who made our already eclectic group even more electric! He was a man with a heart of pure gold, tough as nails, and always willing to go that extra step. As I write this, we recently lost Jim to a long battle with cancer, and, along with his lovely wife, Carol, we all miss him dearly. There'd be no NOVA without the heart and electric soul Jim gave to this baby, NOVA 535. We loved Jimbo.

The experience was a long train of serial "Should we...?" moments, right from the get-go. Should we sell art or only display it? What about the bar? Should we open it to the public or only book it for private events? Who should we target as our primary clientele? We needed to choose interior and exterior colors and select complementary materials, and we needed to do it, like, right away. How should we go about channeling human traffic flow? There were major issues surrounding sound and temperature controls. We had to evaluate our best options for lighting. We needed lighting for daytime art viewing, for evening ceremonies, and for 3:00 AM DJ mash-ups. Those are all very different types of lighting. At one point, I said, "Just make sure it's all on a dimmer." Answers and solutions always had to fit through my filters: world-class, sexy, and timeless. And on a dimmer.

Our hammering and cutting took the building down to its shell and exposed the good bones of the former Pet Planet. We uncovered a gorgeous backdrop for artwork, which allowed me to accent it with beautiful, artistic lighting. Should we make holes in the old girl's Spanish clay tiles so we could hang new artwork each day in different locations for different events? *No!*

We were overwhelmed at times by the demands of decision-making, and the pressure from always having to fit it all into the world-class, sexy, and timeless framework of our new, exciting environment. Design and planning seemed to take longer than the actual implementation of plans. We had to remain true to my vision of an art gallery, a swanky lounge, and an event space, all rolled up into one beautiful package.

Anyone who has braved the renovation of their bathroom or kitchen at home can better understand what we went through. We had to seamlessly integrate an art gallery, a classy bar, a swanky nightclub, a memorable wedding venue, a TV studio, and more, all within one confined space. The most difficult part was that these different venues had to appear on a moment's notice, almost magically. Each unique use had to come to life instantly in a single space and evoke our signature concept.

Have you ever gone into a nightclub on the afternoon following a night out to retrieve a lost phone or perhaps your Visa card? Next time that happens, look down at the floor and underneath the tables and seats (actually, please don't). Disgusting! NOVA 535's lighting, sound, and design features had to communicate an atmosphere that withstood hyper-critical scrutiny under the brightest of shining day-lights.

We needed to preserve the flexibility of our venue for an afternoon TV commercial shoot or a sunset wedding ceremony and reception. Also, if the CEO and her team from a Fortune 500 company rolled in for a corporate dinner meeting and presentation, our venue had to be spotless and have its operating systems Swiss-German tight.

NOVA 535 has since been the scene of countless late-night, wild and crazy, epic, adults-only parties. We built NOVA so that it was tough enough to literally withstand "drunken linebackers." Please come to our annual Halloween costume party, NOVAween, to see what I mean. (Events open to the public are found at NOVA535.com.)

I was fortunate to have support from the right people at the right time. I met a really solid, cool, old-school guy named Chuck Taylor. Chuck is an AV (audiovisual, as well as lighting/sound/video/production) guru, and we quickly became like brothers. I call him Gandalf (the wizard in *The Lord of the Rings*). Check out his website, Production-Source.net. He was instrumental in helping maximize the production values of our audiovisual system. I've learned and continue to learn so much from him. It's like interfacing with an AI (artificial intelligence) who brings teraflops of AV wisdom and relevant—though long (haha!)—stories. Another thank you is owed to my good friend, Chris Skeie, who hooked me up with Chuck. We couldn't have created NOVA without these finest of gents.

I ran up against issues with the lighting and hanging of artwork from our 1920 antique clay block walls. I wanted systems that were strong and flexible because art comes in so many shapes and sizes. Storage space is always a premium at NOVA 535. We first considered using an array of easels for the display of our art. We soon realized, however, that this was a bad call. The floor space from easels kept getting in the way of people and tables. We needed an ingenious design—one that would qualify as an innovative art display system.

Chainsaw Chuck gets the gold star. Yes, another Chuck. That meant our team now had one Emily, two Chucks, and three Mikes. Can you believe it? Chainsaw Chuck was helpful for solving this problem. He is an amazing illustrator. One of the best I've ever met. Although his niche is pin-up girl bondage drawings, Chainsaw Chuck Majewski assured me his images were only of the most willing participants. Not unexpectedly, he applied the intricate wiring, cuffs, and pulleys from his illustrations to our art display conundrum. His creative genius for utilizing mechanical restraints, along with input from me and super-carpenter Mietek Badzinski, produced a unique and compelling display system. It's virtually invisible, super strong, and flexible. (By the way, it is, of course, world-class and sexy. Step into NOVA 535, and I'll show it to you.)

We next designed a logo for signage. To give a boost to our branding, we spent about $7,000 on a gorgeous, custom exterior sign with the words "Art Lounge" in beautiful, bright neon letters. Each letter was flashing to spell out A-r-t L-o-u-n-g-e. It was gorgeous, and it meant we were ready to open.

We scheduled a red carpet opening for February 8, 2009, and the day before, Florida Power gave us a heart-attack level scare when they told us they had made a mistake. "Sorry," they told us, "but we won't be able to hook up your power (today) for your grand opening (tomorrow)."

Talk about being stressed! It seemed like everyone in town was coming. We had delivered Willy Wonka-inspired gold foil with custom-designed chocolate bar invitations to the top one hundred local influencers. Who doesn't love *Charlie and the Chocolate Factory*? And then the only power company in town announced twenty-four hours before showtime, "Hey, guys. Sorry we screwed up, but you're gonna be dark tomorrow." Well, I thought, *Not on my watch, guys. No way.* Our team was on the one-yard line in the Super Bowl, and they had just stripped the ball—it's bouncing around in the endzone. This was *not* going to get away from me. We had gone down the whole field, and it was fourth and goal. We were going to win the game. NOVA 535's red carpet opening was not going to be canceled.

I was frantic. I started calling and begging anyone I could find with the electric company to get a Florida Power crew physically into our alley with their trucks to hook up our power. In my mind, I felt like I was back with Amir and could hear him yelling at me to get my hands up and fight. At this moment, and at this time, the word "no" wasn't part of my vocabulary.

Each time I heard the word "no," it felt just like another of those punches in Amir's gym that he had taught me to keep absorbing. When you fight, you get hit, hard. Head-swelling, bone-aching, painfully hard. So, you learn to take a beating. You can't win by pulling your punches, either. It's a full-contact beatdown. So, I imagined this was the last round in our three-year fight to open NOVA 535. Exhausted, edgy, staggering, dead tired, with dark circles under my eyes, probably wavering into and out of the fringes of lunacy, I wondered, what else could I relate it to? It was like one of Amir's black belt tests.

Ultimately, I tracked down "the guy" at Florida Power who could make the right calls and get shit done. People will make excuses all day, but when it's your business life on the line, you find a way. It was all VA, sans the "NO." After all, we have robots on Mars. I relaxed (a bit) when I watched them hook up the line in the alley. Then the lights and power were on; it was time to party.

(With "Duly Noted" props to my favorite data ninja, Melissa "Mel" Nguyen). Most karate and martial arts schools make money from offering "belt tests" in every color of the rainbow. White, yellow, peach, teal, orange, yadda, yadda. Ask anyone who has taken one of Amir's belt tests how much they paid. In dollars, it's zero. In pain and mental anguish, a fucking ton. You do *not* wanna take his tests; I took two. I failed the first one. In fact, all four of us did. But I went back a few months later and passed the second time. I believe passing that second test (along with opening NOVA 535), was one of the hardest things I've ever done. #YesYouCan.

On opening night, the line stretched literally around the block. NOVA 535 was a packed house with 1,200 guests (Drew counted them all—Thanks, T$), and coincidentally, it was one of my best pals, Danny Pugliese's fortieth birthday. And wow! What a night it was.

Our beautiful hardwood floors weren't installed yet, so we danced on plywood, but no one cared. DJ Zeph flew in from San Francisco and killed it. At midnight, we had fifty gorgeous ladies, all in black, subtly slithering through the crowd, tying the room and the humans in it together in an unforgettable moment as we formally welcomed NOVA 535 into the world. The packed room witnessed the birth of a beautiful new baby venue. #Fatherhood.

Our 1,200 guests kept streaming in all night, and funny enough, just before we opened the doors to guest numero uno, Emily and I were literally carrying in NOVA's infamous red couch (oh, the stories it could tell . . .) into our downstairs parlor directly under our lovely Buddha painting. That night, my mom said, "Wow, honey. You look exhausted." #Understatement.

Touchdown, game over. We won the three-year Ironman Renovation Super Bowl award.

Six months later, we were working hard to become known, shining brightly as downtown St. Petersburg's star attraction: the new NOVA 535 Art Lounge. And, yes, as always, Drew Edwards was there, not so quietly whispering into my ear, "Nobody knows what the *F* an art lounge is."

Event space? Yes, everyone got that. Wedding venue? Of course. Banquet halls? Everyone has been to those. But art lounge? Nope.

This hiccup in our branding was a turning point for us. We did a fast pivot and began communicating the right message. NOVA 535 Art Lounge was soon reborn as a 5-Star wedding and event space: the NOVA 535 Unique Event Space.

Soon after, I began hosting weekly meetings filled with bright, successful Entrepreneurs. I mentor them through my Entrepreneur Social Club every Thursday night. That's been a lot of Thursdays! My advice to them has always been to align naming and branding from the first day. Those are the elements of a business model that need to be clear, concise, and compelling. There should be no mystery or confusion. I followed the smart advice of our team by ditching the "art lounge" moniker.

Thinking back, one of the greatest benefits from nearly twenty years in the world of multi-family investing was that I was able to accumulate properties that provide a reliable passive income stream. The core goal was to lease all my units so I could then (almost) be out of a job. Sure, there was always work and drama. Always! But after a ton of hard, backbreaking work and stress, I had found a wonderful independence. I was in the fortunate position to travel the world for the first time in my life. I told myself, "Okay, I've worked hard, never splurged on fancy clothes or jewelry, and never blown money on expensive hobbies—aside from drinking and playing video games. *Asteroids*, *Missile Command*, *Pac-Man*, and *Donkey Kong* ate enough of my quarters over the years to fill an Olympic size swimming pool. I didn't have a wife, kids, or school loans (thanks, Dad!) and I never had a McDorkstar mansion." So, I took the opportunity to travel and feed my passion for discovery.

I was inspired by new worlds of art, culture, music, food, architecture, and history, which was where so many of my original art lounge concepts and ideas sprang from. It's too bad I lost all those apartments in the great crash, but those adventures abroad were a priceless catalyst that still fuels my creative hyperdrives. As of this writing, I have traveled to eighty-seven countries that have immeasurably enriched my life in so many different ways.

The exposure to ancient and fantastic cultures, people, food, music, landscapes, and histories has been a wonderfully enriching experience. Travel refreshes me and, at the same time, gives me a vehicle to let my naturally hyperactive, inquiring, go-go nature soar into the newness of a once-in-a-lifetime adventure. Traveling gives me the inspiration and fortitude to grow and to navigate the slower-moving things around me.

In the summer of 2017, I was distracted during a trip to South America at an otherwise lovely hotel dining experience in Asuncion, Paraguay. The tiny South American country is Chile's cute little neighbor to the west. (Just kidding, It's to the east. You didn't have a clue, did you?)

I enjoyed my stay at this beautiful hotel, except for two huge floodlights installed in a way that painfully interrupted my vision with a blinding light that utterly ruined my chances of enjoying my dinner. My first night there, I came down from my room anticipating a relaxing meal in a lovely glass-enclosed dining room. After wincing in pain for several seconds, which even the fantastic Rioja could not subdue, I pointed out those menacing lights to the staff—that would be the waiter, the bar-back, and the kitchen manager. Of course, nothing was done. Everybody made me think they already had more than enough to do (yawn), so I concluded they were put off by my shitty Spanish and had placed me in the category of an annoying American. Their attitude was: "We will do this manana, senor." The eternal manana. *Yeah, sure*, I thought to myself. *Sure you will.*

Travel can be a grind on the best of days, and for my second night in Asuncion, I wasn't feeling like hitting the noisy streets for dinner, so I headed back downstairs into that beautiful glass dining room, anticipating a well-deserved and relaxing glass of wine before their delicious local cuisine. The previous night's meal had turned out to be fantastic, and I had enjoyed a dusty bottle of old-world red wine at about 25 percent of what it would have cost at home. After perusing the other dusty racks for a new corky pal to dine with, I made my way into the dining area to be seated. After being shown to my seat by a beautiful hostess (my stammering Espanol es muy malo), I was once again blinded by those intrusive lights. I waited for the hostess to disappear from sight so I could jump out of my chair, dash through the rear exit door, and navigate my way behind the hotel's glass atrium.

I started climbing up the atrium's landscape, while carefully jumping from rock to rock so as to avoid the plants, the flowers, and the blinding light—all while trying not to be noticed by the other guests as a "loco Americano!" They would have wondered, *What's wrong with him?*

Looking back on it, I realize that one might ask me, "Michael, you were leaving the next morning. WTF is wrong with you? You could have just sat somewhere else, dummy." True. I seem to have some crazy compulsion to solve problems. I also have the compulsion to sit in the "best" seat in the house. Every room has a unique energy and flow, and there is always at least one best sitting spot. And for me, at that moment, in that place, I felt it was a mission that called me to action. I was seated in the best spot.

It only took a few minutes for me to adjust those bulbs, and it gave me the satisfaction of making a subtle improvement in the future dining experience of hundreds of pairs of eyes. These tiny improvements, which we can choose to make daily, add up and make things better for all of us. If those around us are better off, then we all are better off. #LeaveItBetterThanYouFoundIt.

What comes to your mind when someone talks about Japan? Ancient but modern? Respectful of nature yet ultra-high-tech? The Japanese have been perfecting the art of excellent customer service for centuries. I say that world-class service is like those rare days when the weather is perfect—when it's so good that it disappears from consciousness. Things just happen seamlessly, providing you with exactly what you need just moments before you consciously think about wanting it.

Ask me about the 5-Star customer service way of life I encountered in Kyoto, Japan! The maids and hotel staff back away from the guests, with the understanding that guests are there to relax and should not be aware of the work the staff is doing. When you see a cleaning lady, you begin to realize the hard work she does, and you understand that she isn't being paid enough. How about your own dirty laundry? (Both kinds.) But in Kyoto, they've been providing 5-Star service for centuries, so they understand the fine, delicate bubble of relaxation—and how easily it can be popped. The Japanese offer food designed, delivered, and presented so beautifully and smoothly that it is a treat to experience and appreciate. Maids and staff literally hide from the guests' sight, even to the extreme of backing out of elevators so that the guests can ride alone. Their job description is to protect the guests' bubble from bursting due to awareness of their work and effort. It's the guests' time to relax and experience Zen. Domo arigato.

That's how it works, I promise you. After reading this book, I hope you will join me in *thinking* about improving even the littlest of things, sort of paying it forward, adding to the collective betterment of our fellow humans. You may want to host 5-Star weddings, parties, and events for a living. If so, then you're fucking nutso like me. But if you do, you will enjoy many laughs along the way. Plus, you'll look at our world a bit differently.

At NOVA 535, we say, "Are you finding solutions or making excuses?" That's the beauty of the NOVA Way. We don't ignore problems, because they aren't going away like the monsters under our beds when the lights turn on. Don't let things fall into the cracks, as Drew says. Be proactive. Think, how can I fix this? It feels good to make things better, doesn't it? Recently, there was a fantastic TV commercial based on how small acts of kindness (improvements), like smiling and saying hello, holding the door open, being kind to a stranger, these "acts" spread outward, maybe even coming back to you (Karma) when you least expect it.

Our NOVA 535 consultant, Nick Mazeika, along with web guru, Chris Jenkins, have been driving forces in helping us develop the NOVA Way. Nick continuously reminds me that we live in a perpetual state of creative destruction. Take it apart and see how much better we can make it. It's a little more work but important in the world of weddings and event planning.

I take the notion of creative destruction as a starting point. Consider the incremental improvements of smartphones. They started as a little piece of plastic, and now we can't live without them. Think about the device you're reading this on. Think of all the inventions we rely on, such as live videos, or speaking to a computer and receiving instant answers to your questions. Technology saves and organizes all the data we desire about our 100,000 closest friends. Only a few years ago, all of that was unimaginable. We are the beneficiaries of a continuous improvement environment that has been made possible by these incremental steps forward.

Chapter 5

Planning and Hosting Your Own 5-Star Weddings, Parties, and Events

t's important to keep a couple of things in mind as you start planning your own 5-Star wedding, party, or event. First off, never overlook the obvious. Why are you throwing the event? If you're lucky, the answer will be self-evident.

I know what you're thinking: *How is life, liberty, and the pursuit of happiness not self-evident?* That rant is contained in a book I keep in my desk drawer with the working title, *The Illusion of Freedom.* I started writing it after grad school, when I was dealing with the laws here in the United States that clearly were *not*

> created to support a free marketplace but seemed more like they were created to protect the few already in power. That, my friends, is another book for another day. Focus, Michael, focus!

Why are you hosting the event? Well, let's consider a few different "whys." For instance, are you hosting a holiday party or maybe an important anniversary celebration? Perhaps your client is hosting a grande quinceañera or a blingy sweet sixteen party. Then again, maybe it's just a traditional birthday or wedding. These different kinds of events seem pretty much transparent in terms of *why* you're hosting them. A word of caution here: There are many types of parties and events that *seem* transparent, but as you begin to dig deeper into the *why*, you can easily get lost and trapped inside layers of timelines, entertainers, multiple dining times and options, speeches, surprises, and—oh shit, it's time to cut the cake! Trust me, things can get murky real fast.

Creating an event can feel like quicksand. You can get drawn in, and once you're in, you may find yourself struggling to find solid ground. I remember a party not long ago that was being sponsored by a New York event company at our NOVA 535 venue. Their event involved a magazine, a liquor company, and a famous DJ. After discussing plans with the host thoroughly and in detail, it was still not clear exactly what they wanted to get out of the event.

The out-of-town clients said their company was "celebrating" the launch of their new product. This was during a time when liquor companies were promoting new flavors, and during this round, everything was "____ & BLACK" or "BLACK & ____." The event had a nice budget, and I was most happy to host it. But if I could have reached a deeper level of clarity, we could have extended the guests' experience from a fun event to a "holy shit, that was an amazing" experience.

The room was ready, our lighting was set to sexy as hell, and we had the DJ's sound checked and ready to roll, all with the power of a high-profile magazine behind us. We provided free, delicious cocktails in a city full of people who love free things and *love* to party. And I mean L.O.V.E. to P.A.R.T.Y.

It's sad to report that our turnout was weak when we should have had a line of the Joneses around the block. I expected to run out of supplies. I know now that I didn't plan well enough to include one simple option: guests could invite guests. That would have transformed what I thought was an "invited guests only" sort of event into telling everyone on the guest list to invite their friends. Because, in the end, it was free drinks for everyone. That was the unknown in the equation; I didn't know then that I should have asked my client if she was okay with guests bringing guests. One simple question stood in the way of greatness. #FailureOfUnderstanding.

Those experiences taught me to take time to dig deep and continue probing until I'm sure that my team and I understand the WHY. Also, while you have your "planner's" hat on, think of a single, clear, and simple message to describe the event.

That big, out-of-state client taught me to find simple solutions for complex problems. To get to those simple solutions, I learned to ask the right questions.

- Why are you throwing this party?
- Can guests invite other guests?
- What promotions are we allowed to do, if any, before the event?

- What are you doing with all the photos, videos, and data afterward?
- Who owns that data?
- Who can use that data? And where, when and how?
- Any other restrictions? Like, does the photographer require the use of his/her watermark? Or can you get clean (no watermarked images?)
- What are your follow-up plans for guests? Do you have their contact (email) info so you can share images, etc.?

After you have answered these questions, you are ready for your invitations, event descriptions, and marketing because you have clearly identified the four "W's."

1. **What** is happening?
2. **When** is it happening?
3. **Where** is it happening?
4. **Why** is it happening?

Here's a quick example.

WHAT:
Sunscreen Film Festival Opening Night Party

WHEN:
Monday, April 20, 2020, from 6:00 PM to 10:00 PM

WHERE:
NOVA 535
535 Dr. M. L. King Jr. Street North, St. Pete, Fl 33701
<Google Map Link to Address>
Parking Details.
If valet, is it free to guests, or should they get their wallets out?
If self-parking, is it metered or free?

WHY:

To Welcome Filmmakers, Cast, Crew, and Fans to St. Pete and get the 15th Annual SSFF Started with a Bang!

Other Important Details:

Is there a dress code? Are there age restrictions? Is there an entry fee? Can invited people bring guests? Will food be served? Will that food be free of charge or available for purchase?

A supercritical element of every event is the bar. Will it be a cash and (hopefully) credit bar? Will you have an open bar? Are drinks free for guests? If yes, what kind of drinks, and for how long? We will touch on these questions in detail later. Can you BYOB? (Typically, that's a no-no, as selling spirits is how many of us pay our mortgage.)

You can expect to encounter clients who want to force their morals—and even some not-so-great dietary and lifestyle choices—on all your guests. That can be fine, depending on the type of event. If you're holding a charity fundraiser, remember this rule: Fundraisers need to be FUN-raisers, and booze needs to be flowing. Why? Buzzed people spend more money. They buy things they don't need but will help a good cause. That's why your three-car garage is so full that you have to park on the street. But is that good for our fragile environment? No, it isn't.

Weddings seem to introduce their own special brand of surprises. I remember one wedding where the mother of the bride was a committed member of Alcoholics Anonymous. She was aghast as she surveyed our bar and demanded that we close it. I told her, "No way." Her request was a non-starter, and I had made it clear from moment one that NOVA's bar never, ever, closes. We keep at least one of our bars open at all times.

Consider this scenario for a moment. Imagine you are traveling by plane to a dreamy, exotic destination. After landing and while waiting to transfer to a connecting flight, you find yourself in the midst of airport terminal chaos, trying to anticipate arriving at your dream destination, which (if you're smart!) is a fantastic vacation here in sunny St. Petersburg, Florida. While waiting for the flight, you understandably develop a thirst for something to help you relax. You're an adult, and maybe, like most folks, flying isn't such a joy. You saunter over to the bar expecting to order a cold beer or a glass of red vino or maybe a whiskey on the rocks. You're undecided, and perhaps you consider a gin martini with a blue cheese olive or whatever. While you savor the anticipation of that relaxing adult bevvy, the bartender walks over to you, wearing a sad frown and an out-of-place, serious expression. He announces disappointingly, "I'm sorry, love. The airport owners don't drink alcohol. We don't serve anything but juice, soda, or tea."

WTF? Hell no! You're a grown-ass humanoid and want a full-strength drink with spirits. In fact, make it a double! (By the way, if you don't want to experience this frustration in real life, then exclude Brunei from your itinerary. I spent a month there one night.)

Your guests are all dressed up and have driven to your venue to spend their precious time, energy, and possibly a lot of money with the expectation of having a great time. They want to feel at home and comfortable. After a few drinks, they want to laugh and talk, very likely a little too loud, and they want to have the 5-Star time they deserve. You can see them making new friends. Their energy is palpable. You can feel it. Their conversations are flowing, and there appears to be a few new romances.

The takeaway is simple. Don't let a guest try to *dick*-tate (not a typo) the terms of other guests' enjoyment.

After throwing over 2,000 events, I can tell you this: It's all about the guests. My goal is always to achieve a tipping point during an event when my guests don't want to leave. I literally want to have to push, pull, and drag people out of the building, way past the last call. When guests would rather stay at NOVA than go home, that is serious confirmation of a great event-hosting experience. It sounds like a fantastic title for a book, maybe something like, ***It's 5 AM Go Home!*** And, funny enough, my follow-up book about epic after-parties can be found at ***Its5amWhatsNext.com***.

In addition to everything else our NOVA events do, they bring people together in one place to share a rare and unrepeatable experience. There will never ever again be that same moment and energy, created by that specific combination of people, in one location, sharing their unique cocktail of energies experienced together.

Each fall, NOVA 535 gears up for our annual adults-only Halloween costume party, NOVAween. We've hosted this annual holiday event since 2007. Though many people attend year after year, it's always a wildly unique experience. So, keep this in mind, the fantastic part of hosting events is the opportunity it gives you to provide your guests with a wonderful incentive to create new connections—possibly deep relationships—in a magical environment, created by you, their 5-Star event host. Those new relationships have the potential to last a lifetime. Shared memories made in the semi-darkness with bass thumping and glasses clinking—those precious moments are never to be forgotten. It's about the laughter, zaniness, and crazy dance moves that make you feel truly alive.

One of my favorite NOVAween Costumes was when I went as Captain Candy. My brother Chris says I often "talk salad." My "niece" Paloma made a reference to the phrase in regard to my quest for a costume—something to the effect that I could go as a big bowl of salad. I pivoted the idea to building a bowl surrounding my body, filled with candies. After the addition of a cape, a face-painted mask, plus two lovely female go-go dancer "costume accessories," we were like Johnny Appleseed sharing candies with our guests. Bold guests, who were good and plenty, could dig down into my candy "pants" and grab handfuls of sweetness. Hilarious! Check out NOVAween.com for photos!

(((Chapter 6)))

Who's Invited?

s this event open to the public? A semi-private affair? Or invite-only?

Open to the Public

Whenever hosting a public event, it's important to know the landscape. "Public" means anyone can attend, although you can specify age limitations, like eighteen or twenty-one, based on liquor laws. Whether you're selling tickets in advance, at the door, both, or not at all, the goal is to achieve what my friend, the infamous "King of St. Pete," Jon "Reno" LaBudde calls "asses in seats." If your public event doesn't attract much of the public, no bueno. People tend to stroll into an event, take a peek, and head straight back out lickety-split if your scene is dead, so the host has to plan and promote public events properly. Typically, you need two to three months' time to properly promote and execute an event that is open to the public.

Advanced planning is even more critical if it's your first event or if the party is about something or someone that isn't well known. Scout the landscape and keep an eye on the calendar. If the event date competes with other events (in most mid-size and larger cities, there's always lots of competition), it's even harder to generate a good turnout. Speaking of which, keep in mind that to get people to show up to your event, you're not just competing against other events—you're competing with every other possible thing people can do with their time. Repeat: You are competing with everything else they could be doing during your event. Look up the term "opportunity cost."

Your guests' preferences, after a long day at the office, may be to just come home (and stay home) after work. Some guests may not feel 100 percent that day, and some may have had a few too many bong hits. There may have been in a big fight with a live-in partner, or maybe the Oscars are airing on TV that night. Think about the hours leading up to the last event you were invited to. At least one item on the list of why not to go certainly danced around in your mind. Maybe you thought about watching Netflix and chilling. There are many reasons not to attend. Maybe that extra-spicy discounted, Mexican, double bur-ree-ta—*no*, you shouldn't have had for lunch, is now no muy bueno.

You can't control shitty weather, but you can plan for it. Marketing plans should include a compelling pitch to entice event guests to brave bad weather if Zeus (Greek god of rain and thunder) dampens your parade. When the gods aren't happy and send thunderstorms your way, forget about it. Only diehard sports fans brave a storm for their team. These days, we can all park ourselves in front of a huge HDTV and hunker down during bad weather.

Speaking of which, did you forget there was a big sports game night? You absentmindedly forgot the playoffs were on that night. Make a reminder to check playoff schedules for hockey, football, baseball, soccer (football to the rest of el Mundo), the Olympics, etc, as they certainly add to the list of reasons guests may use to ditch your event.

Selling non-refundable tickets in advance, with an early bird discount, is super helpful. People are more likely to attend if they have a "rain or shine" financial incentive to attend the event. If the weather gets bad enough, many say, "screw it, I'm staying home," but then at least you have collected a partial return on investment (ROI) from an advance ticket sale. Your bar sales suffer, but some money is better than nada.

We always ask ourselves, "What is a fair price for an event?" Let's say it's $20, and we offer a $20 price for advance tickets online but with a price of $30 at the door. That's a $10 incentive to buy now. You can choose to start at a $15 price for the first few weeks, then go to $20 for your advance ticket purchasers, but remember that most people are lazy and last-minute deciders. So, what's the best advice? Don't bother with tiered pricing, aside from X amount in advance and $X + Y$ percent at the door. So, $20 in advance and $30 at the door.

Nowadays, most tickets are 100 percent digital, no paper, unless you're dealing with some of the old-school venues and corporations. Some promoters like selling paper tickets on the streets, but they are often burned by people printing fake tickets. At NOVA, we like paperless because it's secure and better for the environment. There is a unique code and number for everyone, right there on your phone. Plus, we capture the buyer's data, email, name, etc.

My pal Rainer Scheer displays massive huevos by exclusively hosting outdoor events. His super amazing Chill Lounge festivals are like a spectacular outdoor festival, meets VIP lounge, meets Cirque du Soleil. True, he has been rained on a few times, leaving him with nightmarish stress levels. Luckily, it didn't rain when he married our lovely graphic designer, Patty Filomeno, who rode out on a white horse in the middle of the show. Bravo!

Also, mi bonita amiga, Olga Bof, who is the founder of Keep St. Petersburg Local and throws Localtopia every year in lovely downtown St. Pete, got rained out herself a few years ago, and it nearly broke her. Well, to be clear, although it rained, thousands of us came despite the weather to support Olga. We all love her (and our city of St. Pete, Florida) so much. Still, rainouts diminish chances for profits. Advance, nonrefundable, rain or shine, pre-sold tickets often literally can make or break some events.

If you are not solidly bankrolled, a single unprofitable event can be crushing. Both Rainer and Olga are stronger than ever now because they are true Entrepreneurs with an attitude that says "keep going forward toward success" until their last breath; I love those two. The lesson learned is that outdoor events are for the bold, well-funded, and insane. But when the weather is just right, they are magnificent.

Don't forget to support your local event Entrepreneurs. Even if you just buy one ticket, think of it as investing in your local art scene.

Semi-Private or Plus-One

Another popular event genre is semi-private or plus-one. When you host a semi-private or plus-one event, you generate an invite (guest) list, and allow invited guests to bring one or more friends. These plus-ones can be included with the ticket if it's a ticketed event. Or they may each have to buy a ticket, too. Be aware that this genre will have an unknown number of mystery guests who become added wild cards to your event. Trust me, you should fully expect one of your guests' crazy-ass uncles, or his recently divorced friend, Susie, to show up with the intention of making your event memorable—but not necessarily for the reasons you wanted.

Keep in mind that these semi-private (plus-one) events open the doors to wild and crazy outcomes, sometimes for better and occasionally for much, much worse.

Invite-Only

A third event category is "invite-only," which means just that. If someone ain't on the list, then, sorry sister, they won't be admitted. "Really?"

Well, let's discuss this. I personally have thrown many parties, especially in my younger days, which were invite-only. Except, shit. I realized on the night of the event that I forgot to include one or two of our must-have guests on the list. So, if you're planning an invite-only guest format, decide in advance whether you will enforce it strictly or allow a flexible interpretation of "invite-only."

Invite-Only (Flexible) vs. Invite-Only (Strict)

Understand that these invite-only options require you to make a firm choice and stick with it. It's critical to hire a seasoned, professional doorman with clear, explicit instructions. Invite-only (strict) can still produce some measure of uncertainty for your gatekeeper. Suppose, for example, Leonardo DiCaprio or Oprah Winfrey shows up uninvited. Or the client's parents. Um, then what?

When you host public events, it's best to empower someone besides your door security guy or gal to make these outside-the-rules decisions for you. It's better for you to keep mingling and hosting the event without dealing with embarrassing gatekeeper interruptions, especially when your guests are paying to get in the door. If you are called up to the front, and guests are in the process of paying—and maybe you're a bit buzzed—it's easy to take off your bottom-line-minded businessperson hat and wave them in for free.

You should ask event master, Jon LaBudde, about his days at The Big Catch in downtown St. Pete and his (un) successful policy that had him, Mr. Nice Guy, waving in "friends" for free. It's happened to me, and I now consciously avoid being in the line of sight of my gatekeeper for every paid public event. I learned on those nights that everyone wants to be (or is) one of Mike's best friends.

If the event you're hosting is a wedding, keep in mind that for every extra invitee, the couple will (hopefully) receive a gift. But those extra invited persons also add to the budget: food, booze, desserts, tablecloths, napkins, dinnerware, valet, etc.

Of course, you have to include close family and best friends, aka, "A-listers." Then there are "B-list" people who are invited if money and space constraints aren't a factor. It's great if you can invite everyone on your B-list. That permits an optimum guest list and maximizes your chances for creating a fun and memorable event.

Inviting a Wild Card

There is always the risk of an unpredictable, sometimes loud and inappropriate person, who appears and creates a minor (or worse) scene—otherwise known as a drama queen. This person can be most entertaining and a unique source of chit-chat for guests on the way home. From the host's point of view, it's like watching a toddler walk for the first time. You observe the scene with trepidation while holding your breath with each step out of fear that he is about to stumble and fall. Still, great stories and memories are made from these crazy, unexpected, brick-out-of-the-sky moments.

Stop for a moment and think of a few of your own favorite memories. Remember when you missed a plane, or when the car tire blew out at sixty miles per hour? Ah, those brushes with mortality. Remember the night your friend's crazy cousin (the one we called Duckler) got drunk and was blathering on and on about his recent strip club adventure and subsequent break-up, which, for some inexplicable reason, he could not correlate? He was acting like a complete buffoon. He was loud and annoying, but, at the same time, he was utterly hilarious. You were laughing so hard you almost pissed your pants. These can be the ingredients for your life's great "classic" stories and the memories you and your guests will be telling, and retelling, until your dying days.

In summary, depending on the type of party—wedding, celebration, holiday party, film shoot, cocktail party, dance party or fundraiser—the risks of inviting one or more of these wild card (WC) guests should be considered with your team and partner(s). If a WC guest is okayed, then you've got to discuss how the WC is going to be managed by the host. WC invitees often turn out to be the guests who unexpectedly contribute the most to the success of your event.

Recall the dreaded office parties we all have been subject to. They seem to have all had the same outcome: "Yawn. How can I (gracefully) get the fuck outta here?" You scan the room, hoping to find anyone cool to talk to. If it's a must-attend, then the A-list "cool peeps," like my pal David Hoang, always arrive late. They make everyone laugh and smile. Then you blink, and *poof*! They've blazed away, off to greener fields. The cool kids like Dave stay long enough to grab some food, a few cocktails, some digits, and register minimal face time with the boss and fellow influencers. Then they are off to the real party somewhere else.

It's best to create a "destination" kind of party. Don't be the warm-up, "how can I get outta here" event. Instead, be *The* Party. Or, better yet, become the after party, where the AAA-listers like Hoang hang out. Check out the wildest, most unbelievably epic after-party stories at Its5Am-WhatsNext.com.

To be truly 5-Star, parties need to be fun, memorable, and talked about for months, years, or even decades afterward. Like when Tampa Bay celebrity artists, the Vitale Brothers, produced Size Matters back in 2009. In typical NOVA 535 style, we wrapped their show inside of an extravagant party, with the perfect combination of art, music, and fashion. The all-star lineup was sick. It included Ales Bask Hostomsky, Andrew Spear, Tes One, Terribly Odd, metal master Frank Strunk III, Chris Parks of Pale Horse Design, Sarah Gail Hutcherson, Chad Mize, Phillip Clark, T.W. Curtis (RIP), Ron Pieniak, Heinz Hinrichs, Joey Vitale, Paul Vitale, and John Vitale, and many more. I sure Nick Kekllas was also around, lending a helpful hand. Size did and still does matter.

Investing time into putting together great all-star guest lists is like planning the ingredients for a memorable and unique dessert. Creating the correct mix of people helps yet sadly doesn't guarantee a 5-Star, tasty experience. Do you want Larry from accounting, who photocopied his butt-naked self, and Mary, who passed out on the couch with her face painted by mischievous co-workers? (Yes!)

It helps to have all-stars, but maybe, depending on who you must answer to, not at *any* cost. We had DJ Fresh skateboarding at 5:00 AM all over the dance floor—the first of many crazy birthday parties he threw at NOVA 535. Dougie rolled in one year, literally driving onto our dance floor in a $250K custom convertible Mercedes, filmed live. Showstopper. My consultant pal, Amy Miller, invaded our venue with her badass roller derby girls in tow and had her most memorable of birthday parties. Think South Beach Lounge meets Live Roller Derby. Good thing both DJs were willing to extendzzz.

The goal is to capture the kind of behavior that is recalled, even somewhat hazily, decades later with a smile. Create memorable events. Invite a wild card or three. People want a boring party as much as they want dry-ass chicken.

(((Chapter 7)))

The Big Date

Some brides obsess over a specific calendar date that they just gotta have for their wedding. It's usually hopeless to argue about the date she has chosen for her wedding, though we do try.

From the event host's point of view, dates are just numbers on a calendar. Sometimes, a bride can be flexible, and that's fantastic. When you're responsible for planning and hosting a wedding, you carry a unique set of obligations to make it a success, and your responsibilities are different from the bride's.

For starters, you want a date that works for the A-listers because those are your core must-have peeps. Take care that the date doesn't conflict with other major events that can negatively affect your attendance. The couple's family can have private traditions that might conflict with a specific date, and the only way to know is to ask. Also, if you're not an avid sports fan, please ask friends about big matches you are clueless about. Some brides are cool with having "the big game" on TV during their reception and may be front and center to watch it themselves. Many, though, are definitely not cool with guests watching "third and long from your own fifteen." Understand your clients. Then you will know exactly how to delight them!

You must tread delicately, as weddings involve two people getting married—two people and their families. They can be very different types of people. So, the bride/partner can be saying TVs are off, and the groom/partner can be saying TVs are on, while mom-in-law can be saying it's up to her since she's paying the bill. We have four unique spaces at NOVA 535, which means we can quietly put the game on upstairs while the main event happens below. Everyone is happy . . . until that special someone is found glued to the game and *not* to their newlywed partner. #NewlyWedFight1.

Whatever day of the week your wedding or event falls on, Monday, Friday, etc., usually isn't a problem in and of itself. However, if some of your guests can't or won't attend because of personal scheduling conflicts, then that suddenly becomes an issue for you. Give your guests time to plan so they avoid those kind of personal scheduling conflicts. Weddings and big events should be scheduled twelve to eighteen months in advance whenever possible. That's plenty of time for your key peeps to reschedule when necessary. If it's a birthday celebration, then obviously, the event date needs to be close to the actual birthday. It doesn't have to be on that day, but it makes things extra nice when it is. If people really want to attend your event, they will. #ExcusesOrSolutions.

For a New Year's Eve or Valentine's Day celebration, yeah, that actual date matters. See if there is an opportunity to negotiate and clear any self-imposed limitations by your client, such as, "Oh, it's got to be on a Saturday," or, "The bride's age and wedding date have to add up to twenty-seven because my horoscope requires it." Hogwash. Press on and suggest an alternative. Subtly suggest that their magical formula for the date really interferes with the success of her event. Smart promoters like Doug Hensel (DJ Fresh), Jeff Copeland, and Jon LaBudde understand their audiences and how to promote and throw an event on a Wednesday that'll have lines waiting out the door. For example, don't throw a New Year's Eve (NYE) party on NYE for industry people (bartenders, bar-backs, waitstaff, cooks, chefs, hostesses). Throw it the following Tuesday or Wednesday night, when all the industry people are mostly off. Don't forget to thank (that means tip!) and celebrate all the hard work that our industry folks do, day in and day out.

Depending on the type of event, weather can be a nuisance. Even a nightmare. As we've heard, "It's not nice to fool with Mother Nature." What's great about NOVA 535 is our expansive, open-air brick and bamboo courtyard. We can set up our parties and wedding ceremonies outdoors. Then, if Ma Nature has other plans, it's only a few steps, and the guests have a protected safe haven inside our beautiful historic venue. You can always rent a tent, but that involves significant expense and planning, and tents can be stuffy and unwelcoming. The grand ones cost several thousands of dollars, though they can be a necessity and made to be gorgeous (like how our pals at U.S. Tent Rentals do things).

143

Planning for Fuck-Ups!

One thing I stress over even with our NOVA safeguards in place is the occasional double-booking error. When your venue or planning business is in demand, and it's the middle of wedding season chaos, it's possible for you to screw it up royally and tell two brides, "Sure, you can have Tuesday night, October 20, 2020, for your special wedding day! That's no problema." Then, a few hours later, your team catches up with the error, and someone announces that we're gonna have to eat a big pile of crow and notify one of the brides that we have to reschedule her special event.

I've had to make that call a few times, and I fucking hate it. We all make mistakes, and the more complex your system is, the more you make. Keep things as simple as possible, and double check before confirming dates. Almost anything else is fixable, but two brides wanting the same date leads to lots of stress dreams and headaches for everyone involved. I know. I've had to nut up and make those calls. #LoseLose.

In your planning, pay special attention to the client's wedding or event theme. Formal events often require formal dress and are fantastic with cool and temperate weather, but they can be brutal in the summer swamp season in Florida. Wearing long dresses and tuxes in 95-degree weather, with 70 percent humidity, is a nightmare. Some guests will suck it up for their bestie, but the whole time they're thinking, "I wanna choke someone, then hang myself."

Summertime in the Sunshine State is challenging at best, and when you throw kids into the mix, managing those energetic, noisy little munchkins really turns up the heat. For some insane reason, no one has developed a revolutionary babysitting app like "Uber Child" or "Kidsbnb" to help manage transportation and temporary safe lodging for kids. Well, maybe there are apps, but no one has solved the "trusted like grandma babysitter dilemma" yet. Where are all my fellow Entrepreneurs?

Good, reliable babysitters are scarce and not always available for the dates required. Your guests can become uncomfortable committing to a wedding or event date because of childcare issues. Ask wedding planner extraordinaire, Ruby Thomas Dolce, about juggling life, work, and children. If your event is not planned the NOVA Way—with childcare planned way ahead of time—guest attrition occurs with the protestation, "We can't make it because the kids _____ (insert excuse)."

In my long experience throwing professional events, the number-one reason people don't show up is, you guessed it, their "issues" with kids, whether genuine or just convenient. It's best to have your client get a sitter or confirm they have well-behaved kids who can attend the event.

Just get a sitter. Kids will be kids! Ever see *Home Alone*? I've hosted too many events where the kids ended up creating utter chaos, running out on the dance floor during the bride and groom's first dance. I had a dad look at me in utter despair, sigh, and then admit that he had lost control years ago. I blinked and saw him again, at the bar, ordering a double. My parents would have restricted me if I had ever dared to act up at a party or event—not that they would have ever taken me in the first place. Kids and adult parties were, to that generation, like oil and H2O.

My personal favorite day for events at NOVA is Thursdays. I find that everyone can bounce right through Friday after a late-Thursday-nighter. Friday nights seem to go best when I'm home recuperating, working all day on my computer, followed by a home-cooked meal and a movie. Then Saturday can be another big night out. I say that people are too physically, emotionally, and financially exhausted to do anything on Sunday nights. Of course, I'm not twenty-one, either. There is a strong Sunday Brunch party group in DTSP, likely down at one of Steve and Nancy Westphal's delicious restaurants (check out DowntownStPete.com).

Mondays are a strong, no-way Jose. Tuesdays are great because some people have an itch early in the week to party, and there usually isn't a lot of competition on Tuesdays. Also, vendors usually discount for weekday events. Wednesdays are something of a wild card and always seem weird to me because of hump day and all that. Nothing personal—I just seem to prefer Tuesdays and Thursdays for doing stuff during the week, probably because the weekends are always so busy and Thursday nights are my Entrepreneur Social Club. But for Entrepreneurs and small business owners, the work week is any day that ends in "Y."

A quick recap here. Choose the best time of year (season) for your event, unless it's a 100-percent indoors event, in which case, seasonality almost doesn't matter. Of course, no event is 100-percent inside, since you and your guests travel to the venue, unless you are living in the attic/basement (weirdo). And you don't have to worry about exact day-and-date harmony unless you schedule something on Christmas, Valentine's, or Labor Day.

Make sure your most important guests and approved vendors are good with your date. Ultimately, it's all about the people you select. I've had incredible times standing in an alley with the right people. Ask our Entrepreneur Social Club about our alley adventures. Especially that alley behind Chef Jason and wife Hope's fantastic Brick and Mortar Kitchen. Wow, their food is fresh, unique, and delicious. So, let me "alley" your event-planning anxieties and fears. Just follow the NOVA Way when hosting your own amazing 5-Star wedding or event.

Chapter 8

Picking the Perfect Location

When a decision is made to get married or host an event, and the time of year has been chosen, the next item on the agenda is a venue. Location is a critical step for planning the wedding (or event) of your dreams. I call this phase of planning, "Mate, date, and locate." It's critical to manage the details of your event so that you have a venue nailed down and a date locked up with an executed (signed by both parties) contract and payment terms agreed on—first.

A deposit implies that things are still voidable and monies refundable if things don't work out. Be careful about using the word "deposit" instead of "payment." Payments are typically non-refundable. You pay in full (nonrefundable) for a pizza no matter if you throw it in the trash can or finish every last delicious bite. A payment made to NOVA 535 is nonrefundable, which is clearly stated verbally, on our website, and in writing. When we're in, we're both all-in.

It's okay to have a list of preferred vendors already in mind, but until there is a fixed date with a venue, there is no way to be sure of their availability. So, repeat after me. "Mate, date, locate." I'm not going to help you with the mate part, aside from suggesting this: Be a good honest communicator and a patient listener. Always be kind while sticking to your core beliefs and principles. If you are healthy and she is a cigarette smoker, then this is what can be called a structural issue. Party boys and choir girls aren't a good long-term match either. Maybe for a long weekend of sin-ggg-ing lessons; just don't let Sister Nofunatall find out.

Picking the right venue is super critical for your event's success. Unless you're like me and plan these events for a living, there are many things you *will* forget. For example, it's easy to take for granted that a venue has nearby parking. What exactly is nearby? A two-minute leisurely walk or a seven-minute sprint? Is the parking free or paid? Paid how? Bills or coins? Is there a time limit on said parking? Have you confirmed that the venue is air-conditioned? Is the air conditioning provided by moldy, noisy window units or a big, quiet central HVAC system? Is there high-speed (Wi-Fi) internet in all rooms? Spotty coverage will lead to sad-face emojis. Did you confirm that the restrooms are large enough to turn around in without touching the walls? Check everything yourself.

Venue Design Flexibility

With careful evaluation of the venue, you can discover how well your guests fill flow through the facility. Sure, sometimes you want people all cramped up and close to create that hot, pheromone-induced interaction. The kind that invites attraction and random swapping of energy.

Speaking of, is the dance floor the right size? There are times when you will want plenty of room for guests to relax and enjoy themselves. See for yourself that it's everything you want for your event. Think through your guests' (the event "users") experience. When they walk in, will things be cramped? How will it feel during the event from your guests' POV?

Our first NOVA event was hosted by the lovely Helen Hameroff with help from her (new) hubby Franz. It was to celebrate the fortieth birthday of her eldest son, Dr. Dan. Dan was my UF college roommate, an amazing guy who was always willing to share his liquid paper, which I always needed thanks to my many (focus Mike, *focus*!) mistakes. (Liquid paper is the pre-internet delete button. Look it up). Helen taught me much about decorating, layout, and flow, all through her incredible planning, design, and execution of her son's fabulous birthday dinner party. It was in our upstairs area at NOVA lounge. We had about fifty or sixty guests, and she had everything laid everything out perfectly. I was awed. Her other son, the third Dr. Hameroff, Brian, and their father (Helen's ex-hubby), Dr. Nathan Hameroff, plus many other close, amazing friends attended. I couldn't have been happier to host our first event for this lovely family who were surrounded by people who really loved and cared for each other.

That is the core reason to do all this work and stress over something that lasts only a few hours. It's to create those rare moments with friends together, as a family, sort of as a single organism feeding and enjoying the combined love and energies. It makes all the planning worth it. Keep that in mind when you reach that "fuck it, I quit" breaking point during planning. Think about the smiling faces, the hugs, and the laughter. You enjoy the shared love as much as your guests do . . . maybe even more. And many times, that's the best and only thanks you will get. But not in this case. The Hameroffs are beyond gracious.

Some venues have small rooms scattered within their space that create frustrating bottlenecks. They can appear to be maze-like obstacles where you can lose your friends and yourself, but not in a good way. There are important reasons to anticipate problems for your guests, who have to deal with guest-flow bottlenecks. I can think of several issues: getting to and from the bar, waiting to pee, lines that are way too long at the buffet, and vendors annoyingly pushing their way through people to deliver drinks and to clear space for those inevitable cleanups.

Did you check to see that bars and bathrooms are easily accessible and convenient? At NOVA 535, we built the max number of restrooms possible. We have a total of ten restroom suites. Yes, suites! There are six restroom suites downstairs and four upstairs. We were diligent in providing plenty of places to take care of business. Plus, we were way ahead of the curve on (not) labeling them men, women, or none-of-your-business. At NOVA, our guests are humans. They don't need labels. Why should we care who is using the rooms? Just be clean about it.

The funny thing is, I got a call one afternoon while walking my fur babies, Maxwell and Malcolm. The caller (a man) said that NOVA 535 had been nominated for their "Best Restrooms in the USA" award. I laughed because I thought it was a joke, having never heard of such an award. He convinced me that this was a serious accolade in the hospitality landscape and to hold tight for the final results.

Ultimately, we finished in the top ten best restrooms in the United States. The award was sponsored by the giant global corporation, Cintas, and we competed with,

I believe, 5 million other candidate-restrooms. I told my friends, "We really flushed the competition away."

Thinking back on our Best Restrooms in the USA award, our décor is something that showcases the difference between good, really good, and world-class. The thought occurs to me: Where in the world—and I mean where, *anywhere* in the world—as part of your experience have you ever been escorted around for a tour of the restrooms? Well, okay, maybe in a friend's home when they point one out so you know where to conduct business. But seriously, we labored over eliminating (pun) every detail that could possibly make the restroom experience (wait for it) a shitty one. Come take a pee and see for yourself. #WhiteGloveClean.

Parking

Please remember to try not to overlook the obvious. How far away is the parking? Do guests have to wear hiking boots? Is the parking lot area paved? Is there a mud hole if it rains a little? Is it illuminated for safety, or is it pitch black? Do guests park free, or is it metered? Who has seventeen quarters, anyway? Suppose it's raining. Maybe the date of your event is freezing cold.

Getting lost or mugged while your guests are trying to make their way from the parking area to the venue is a catastrophe you want to prevent your guests from experiencing. Worse yet, suppose your guests can't find a place to park, and they collectively decide to let out an exasperated cry of "fuck it" and go elsewhere, like over to that cool, cranking little bar they noticed earlier while trying to park for your event. Yup, stuff like that happens all the time. I bet you've done that yourself. I know I have.

151

Bathrooms

Bathrooms are a delicate subject that is often discussed only briefly—except for event hosts whose standards are 5-Star. So, let's review this important subject for a #2 time.

How many are there? Are they roomy and clean, or disgusting? For a laugh, check out my restroom website Shite. Show. Are your guests spending more time waiting to pee or, god forbid, take a shite? Is there fresh air circulating? Are they quickly and happily refreshed and heading back to the bar and dance floor? Are the toilets in good working order, and do they flush every single time? How many of us have stood there, waiting and hoping that the toilet flushes everything down? OMG.

Do the stall doors have locks? Can you tell that the door is actually locked? Where are you going to set your drink down in there? Hmm. . . . That's happened to me. You certainly don't want to set anything on the floor. Gross! Is there a hook for ladies to hang their purses? How about for the guys' jackets or hats? You hope there is a mirror, maybe even a full-length mirror. Is there plenty of toilet paper, two-ply?

We thought through every conceivable bathroom inconvenience and made it our business to eliminate them. We even added music. Forgive me, but please don't give your guests a shitty restroom experience. #BestBathroomsInUSA.

Lighting

Lighting is a super-duper-critical component for every successful event. It helps create those warm and cozy feelings. No matter whether you're hosting a three-hundred-person wedding ceremony and reception or a thirty-person intimate dinner, in my opinion, lighting makes or breaks an event atmosphere. Check to confirm that overhead down-lighting isn't falling into a guest's eyes. Not ever. No one wants a rogue light flashing in their eyes. Not even in Asuncion, Paraguay. Direct the lights at objects, not people. Indirect lighting is your best friend.

Adjust lighting against paintings on walls to ensure that hanging artwork is perfectly framed. Candles? You can never have too many candles (in glass votives, with the flame two to three inches below the top of the glass). We use fifty-hour oil candles placed inside clear glass votives. For every kind of event, primordial fire is at once invigorating and calming for guests. Your candles should be placed in a way that is engaging, warm, and harmoniously random. It's a simple, powerful, and inexpensive way to make your event feel comfy and relaxing while adding life and energy.

What about the color spectrum of your lighting? Yes, color spectrum. Where on the warm to cold range does it fall? LEDs are the current craze, and yet, most of them are cold—not like the warm yellow of sunlight. Also, do your lights dim? Bet ya' they don't. Sure, super-bright lighting is great for taking your college entry exams, but not at party time. You don't want guests asking you to turn the lights down, please.

The number-one piece of advice for businesses, either those operating in the swanky landscape or those serving dinner and drinks, is simple: Turn down the overhead lights. Get the lights out of your guests' eyes, with more indirect lighting, please. Light up what I need to see, not me. Make sure the proper color spectrum, from cooler to warmer, is chosen. Ask yourself this question: "Is this a jewelry shop or a romantic wedding venue?" Everything in the same room should be on the same color spectrum, and *all* lighting should be on a dimmer. Like Dr. Dan Hameroff's rule: "I want blue cheese on my blue cheese," and I want dimmers on everything.

 Have the venue turn on *all* the lights, and make sure they are the same color, as it's even more annoying (and rookie) to have some cold and some warm, all in the same space. Chuck Taylor of Production Source taught me about the color spectrum, and I love him dearly for that and his many other AV lessons.

Sound Systems

Check every area of your venue to see and hear that a professional sound system is ready to go. I'm often shocked as I travel and visit local wedding venues and event spaces. Many are terrible. Think of a cheap cruise ship lounge. Ugh! Picture all the events you have been to where they jam a DJ behind a six-foot, linen-covered table. The DJ has two ugly-ass speakers, usually on tall stands about eight-feet apart with blaring music drowning out every conversation in that zone.

At NOVA, our guests experience professional, enjoyable sounds. Make them turn on the sound system(s) and go listen to every speaker. Or not. Because who cares if one-third of your guests can't hear anything and another one-third are deaf by cake cutting, right?

Remember that the 5-Star event business is comprised of two parts. It starts with the physical (building and systems). And then there are people (humans) who run things. We humans have ears, and when we go to enjoy a party or an event, hearing is a foundational part of an enjoyable experience. Like Goldilocks, we expect it to be just right. Not too loud so screaming is all you hear, and not too soft so there's no groove to dance to. Sound is shared in many tones, notes, and frequencies, from highs and mid-ranges to lows, down to deep bass. Well, we humans—the techies, the venue manager, the event's DJ, etc.—all need to be paying attention to how sounds from every area and direction are received by our guests.

I found this out the hard way. One night, a new cleaning crew member was under the stairs and unknowingly knocked the plug out from a massive subwoofer bass speaker. That night, the music sounded weird, and people weren't dancing as much. Of course, our clean team, led by James, Shawn, and Craig, would never let that happen again, but sometimes, we have to deal with hundreds of people each week. Many are new, untrained vendors, and it's easy to accidentally unplug or break something. Part of our team's training is to pause, smell, look around, and listen. How is the room temp? What will your guests smell? How is the lighting? Can you find any dirt, filth, crumbs? And does the music sound just right?

I've been lucky enough to work with legendary music gurus and dealmakers like Tom Gribbin, Johnny Green (RIP), Bill Edwards, Rob Douglas, and Chuck and Tracy Ross, who expect things to be just right. If not, they won't be bringing their big regional and national acts to me again.

One of our magical events was hosting the Tampa Bay Blues Fest Official After Party, two years in a row. They are the best collection of blues musicians anywhere and are brought here annually by founders Chuck and Tracy Ross. Since 1995, their Blues Fest has been a headliner here in downtown St. Pete. They are amazing people, and I'm grateful to Tom Gribbin for introducing them to me. The feedback we got was that NOVA 535 sounded better than the House of Blues. That reminds me, the only places in our venue without house speakers are the kitchen (the chef needs to be heard clearly) and within our SUPERNOVA Suite, which has its own private AV system.

The SUPERNOVA and Get-Ready Suites

VIP guests expect VIP treatment, and for them, we have the SUPERNOVA Suite and a beautiful second Get-Ready Suite. Determine in advance where your VIP guests will be getting ready. Does your venue have suites for everyone to prep in?

Our VIP suites have a private entrance and exit, so special guests, entertainers, and bridal parties can come and go without being accosted by fans or their guests. Our two world-class and sexy get-ready suites eliminate the need for a daytime hotel, which can be a lot of unnecessary wasted time and expense, plus all the hassle of traveling from a hotel to the venue. Oh, and traveling usually involves forgetting something, fighting traffic, stress, delays, more stress, etc. The SUPERNOVA Suite sports a gorgeous, all-Italian travertine shower, just in case. (Our guests expect to be showered with 5-Star experiences.)

When preparing for a VIP experience, make sure there are plenty of hooks and hangers for dresses and jackets. Check the private shower and bathroom. Are they clean? What if you're running late and need to change clothes for your big career awards presentation? Look for a venue with a private, luxurious get-ready shower suite like our SUPERNOVA Suite. Is there a secure place to lock up gifts? Does it have a digital combo lock? It's almost like you have to think of *everything*. Pretty much. Yup.

In anticipation of the inevitable hilarious, embarrassing, and droll speeches that are part of the fun, be sure to confirm that the sound system is adequate, so everyone can hear clearly and at a comfortable volume. Don't let the experience turn into a tortuous affront to your guests' eardrums. You don't want guests to miss great storytelling, but neither do you want them to feel like it should end after the first minutes because their ears are ringing like an atom bomb just unloaded next to them. You won't miss a beat at a 5-Star venue like NOVA, even if you're powdering your nose, because the restroom suites are wired for sound.

BTW, I have to ask if powdering noses is still "a thing." I'll ask our NOVA neighbors, Alin and Caylin, (yes, their names rhyme), who hang at Dollylocks Salon. They are incredibly talented makeup artists and delightful ladies.

HVAC

What is HVAC? HVAC stands for heating, ventilation, and air conditioning. Okay, almost everybody assumes your venue is maintained at perfect temperatures and the HVAC runs quietly. Ha! Yeah, sure. The truth is, even the best AC systems can be under-engineered when hundreds of hot bodies are jammed together into a single space for hours on a ninety-plus-degree day.

Air conditioners can run to maintain the (ambient = room) temperature they're set for, then shut off automatically (setting = auto) based on what temperature the thermostat is set to. They can be set to (ON) to let the fan continuously run by itself (even after the thermostat set temp has been reached). Regardless of the temperature settings, people in different parts of the room can experience temps that vary as much as ten degrees above or below the thermostat setting. We all have experienced a hot spot in one part of a room, as well as that uncomfortably cold area just a few tables away.

We thought long and hard on how to prevent that kind of thing at NOVA 535. We installed four inches of a special foam insulation board between our wood deck and the rolled roofing system. And, as we are as green and clean as possible, we designed our multiple HVAC systems to heat and cool NOVA 535 to maximize guests' comfort, while utilizing as little electricity as possible by using three-phase electric and always keeping Mother Earth in mind. Plus, we have a Big Ass Fan [™] with adjustable settings that make a huge difference.

The big ceiling fan's subtle-to-strong air movement keeps the room temperature uniform. So, when our gallery area is packed with four hundred sweating people dancing and having a blast, everyone is comfy. That gets tested during our monthly First Friday Parties, which feature our wild superstar combo DJ Spank and DJ Chill, expertly managed by my charming brother, Chris Novilla, and hosted by the legendary, one and only Jeff "Grown Folks" Copeland. When we crank our Big Ass Fan up to its maximum setting, it literally blows the skirts up! Oh, Marilyn!

Safe to say, that fan keeps us from having to set our air conditioning thermostat down to a ridiculously low temp. Freezing hands and feet prompt a flight response, unless you're from Yukon, provoking thoughts of a fast exit from the building instead of allowing people to enjoy themselves and spend more cash at the bar.

I had a fantastic trip to Canada once where I met a lady who owns a Canadian Pacific train caboose that she painted a beautiful red. She parked it on the side of a majestic cliff overlooking the ocean and converted it into her home. She wrote a book about it, which I purchased and read. (Supporting my fellow Entrepreneurs!) You see how easily I can get distracted. She did give me something like two quarts of fresh blueberries—delicious and so healthy!

Bars

Check the number of bars at your venue. What you really need to ask is, "How many wells are there?" What's a well? Well, a "well" is the station where bartenders work. An (ice) well is chock full of (hopefully) clean, fresh ice for drinks. Make sure the ice machine has enough capacity for your event, and check that the water is filtered. Unfiltered water makes drinks taste terrible. Don't get me started about what poisons are in the water. And do not forget to ask when the last time their ice machine was cleaned and the filter was changed. Ice machines are notorious for never being cleaned. Sucio! Seriously. Lift up the bin cover, take out your smartphone flashlight and don't be surprised if it's N.A.S.T.Y. We clean ours regularly throughout the year and use only filtered water. We go one step further. We look and professionally clean behind the maintenance panel that covers the machinery and water coils behind the machine as well.

The well will (should) be supplied with mixers. Typically, many of these are dispensed with a Wunder-Bar gun. This is found in upscale or permanent bar installations. Our gun at NOVA 535 dispenses Coke, Diet Coke, Sprite, ginger ale, soda water and tonic, tea—both unsweetened and raspberry sweetened—plus staples like cranberry juice, sour mix, and lemonade.

Be sure to confirm that the bar has this system for any large party. It's way faster, and if they are using high-quality products like we have at NOVA, then the consistency and taste of your drinks will be great. You won't (or shouldn't) find orange juice, tomato juice, root beer, or anything heavily acidic in those guns since they scar the interior of the dispensing hoses. We keep certain juices like orange, pineapple, lime, tomato, and a few others in cans or plastic mixer containers to serve directly. They can be kept cold right at the ice well during the event.

Some bars stock one and two-liter plastic bottles, and they go flat quickly. NOVA prefers mini metal cans for grapefruit and pineapple juices because they only hold enough juice for one to three drinks each and stay fresh for weeks, vs. the day or so with two-liters. Here is my soapbox moment: Plastic pollutes our oceans. Fish (and sea life) ingest all those plastic poisons, and then we eat the fish. Less disposable plastic equals a healthier planet. #EliminatePlasticWaste.

When your professional bartenders have the right tools, including proper training, experience, and attitudes, they can provide great service. They each need their own ice well. With the right equipment and ice available, they can be responsible for supplying the stations with clean ice, plenty of mixers, fresh-cut fruit, etc. You should also have a bottle cooler close by for beer and wine, although, if they are both on draft, the cooler isn't necessary. Vino on draft? No. I'm not crazy.

Europeans have had wine on draft for decades. I believe that eventually our politicians will be forced into allowing this throughout the United States as well. Why? Well (haha), it's less expensive, there's less waste, and, obviously, it's much better for the environment. Why isn't it here already? Certain suppliers have lobbied lawmakers to protect their non-draft products, and as those suppliers grow bigger and make more money, they "buy" the laws they want. Can you say, "anti-competitive, anti-free markets"? The system is good for a few but bad for the rest of us. Where is my soapbox?

I have been blessed to have visited eighty-seven countries so far. Ya wanna know the single problem they *all* have in common? Their politicians line their own pockets. Hmm. Maybe it would be better if Entrepreneurs ran the show. Replace the greed, corruption, and waste with transparency, kindness, sustainability, full education, green products and energy, and so on. Maybe create a new system with the same rules as my Entrepreneur Social Club. No religion, no politics, no liars, no bullies, and no thieves. And no peeing in the pool. It has worked great for us since 2009. Really, we need to think of a new operating system for humanity.

Back on track. Our bartenders are stocked with a generous supply of clean and polished glasses, and I promise you we don't use plastic. Joe "Budious" Gray is a legendary lounge designer, a super cool guy, and a good friend of NOVA. Joe told me, "Glass is class, baby!" He created one of the swankiest lounges of all time, Budious Maximus, in Downtown St. Pete. It was way ahead of its time. Joe is a fellow visionary, and I've been to many after parties with Joe. My next book, **It's 5 AM What's Next?** will be interviews about legendary after parties by super cool cats like Joe Budious who have contributed to many of the smart decisions and unforgettable moments we made here at NOVA 535. Love ya, Joe!

There are some occasions when single-use cups are needed, especially if you are far away from a dishwasher and have a huge three hundred or four hundred-person crowd. Some dishwashers can't handle that size of a crowd. Please, for the sake of us all, use one of the many eco-friendly, plant-based alternatives. Or provide each guest with one cup for the entire evening, explaining the reality of our critically fragile ecosystems and that their health is 100 percent our responsibility.

Transportation

Driving to and from any event involves finding a parking space, which is always frustrating. Pay close attention to issues around transportation and parking. City street parking may be free in the late evenings, but it is metered during daylight hours. Will guests and VIPs run out and feed the meters? Or can they relax and enjoy your event? Speaking of parking, we always strongly suggest that our guests rideshare to and from the event and skip the hassle of driving, parking, and walking to the venue—and the meter-feeding headaches.

There are things that some guests may want to bring to the party. Maybe a flask of whiskey, perhaps some smoky-smoke, or whatever they may use as a personal social anxiety crutch. Watch out for Johnny Law. It's important to have door security screen for such things. I lost my ass on an event with a crooked promoter who snuck in a whole bunch of bottles and was selling them (for a while) right under my nose. Guys like that (fucking thief, liar, scumbag) who I'd given opportunities to—and who I invited into my home and my NOVA family—decided to screw me. Still, to this day, he has never repaid me a nickel. Make sure that security is yours, not theirs, and that your guys do a two-person pat down and check everyone. And I mean *everyone*. Bags and purses alike, clients and vendors, too. Watch all entry points, as the kitchen and back alleys are ripe for exploitation.

In the olden days—and even today in parts of the world without rideshare apps—if guests aren't driving themselves, they are stuck having to schedule a taxi or a limo for the event. When I was visiting Nepal in the summer of 2018, with my girlfriend Huyen, there was no ridesharing available. Most everyone had a smartphone in their hand, yet there were nada rideshare apps to be found. Taxis across the globe mostly offer terrible service—overcharging and featuring confusion as to where to go, rude behavior, gross interiors, and drivers smoking cigarettes, screaming into their phones, and swerving wildly. Thankfully, these are, thanks to my fellow Entrepreneurs, rapidly being replaced by modern, convenient, paperless, more reliable, and reviewable transportation rideshare apps.

For the record, the taxi drivers in Kathmandu were surprisingly honest, and most were excellent drivers. I remember one taxi ride I had in Nepal last year. There was a cow running down the middle of the street, but that wasn't even close to the craziest part. Search "Michael Scott Novilla" on YouTube and enjoy watching the "Mike's Crazy Taxi Rides" series, especially my experiences in Kathmandu. You won't believe it!

Some guests are good at convincing themselves that they'll only have one drink and then drive themselves home. Our doorman and security team needs to be alert and to call rides for such guests. For twenty dollars or less, they can get a safe, easy, door-to-door solution for the guest. I speak from personal experience. As I previously mentioned, in 2008, after the Great Recession, when my Lexus lease expired, I chose to turn my Lexus back into the dealer and called a friend to get home. My friends thought I was nutso—including my good buddy and mentor, Drew Edwards. A decade later, I still haven't owned another car. Just a bicycle. I rethought my personal transportation priorities and chose to be car-less. I like being a renter of transportation services, and then, only when I need them.

My transportation costs have decreased by over 50 percent. This isn't even factoring in the soft costs like health and liability reductions. The stress and frustrations of owning a vehicle have disappeared. What's the cost of petrol today? How much is parking? Where can I get my car washed? My response is always, "Who cares?" I get door-to-door service while I work or relax in the back seat. Plus, the super benefit here is my lack of exposure to liability. From the rear passenger seat, I am the client of a transportation company with zero liability for any accidents. My financially savvy friends agree that it's a smart deal.

After your guests are safely ensconced in your venue, you're free to relax and let your hair down, assuming you have any left. (Mine is slowly trying to leave my scalp, though some natural remedies, including shampooing less, seem to have stemmed the tide. Enjoy the moment.)

Back of the House

Does your venue have a well-equipped kitchen? Confirm that the event space has at least a catering kitchen, if not a full kitchen. What's a catering kitchen, you ask? A catering kitchen has an oven(s), sink(s), prep areas, refrigeration (often limited), hot water, a mop sink, an ice machine, and a dishwashing machine. A full-service restaurant kitchen, by contrast, has major equipment like fryers, grills, exhaust hoods, plenty of refrigeration, maybe even a walk-in cooler, etc.

When we outfitted NOVA 535, there wasn't enough physical space for the restaurant-style kitchen. Trying to manage a real-deal food company would have been a disaster. It's easy to remake my guests' vodka tonic, but overcooking one hundred steaks is game over.

Early on, I was fortunate to work with one of the best caterers—and humans—I've known. She is Kate Holway, from our neighboring state of Georgia. Kate taught me so much about food service and the event biz. Wow. Kate cooked for over two hundred people out of our catering kitchen, cleaned up, made deals on the phone, gave prospective clients a warm, welcoming and tour of NOVA, and remained smiling and enjoying herself every moment. Working with Kate was like getting a master's degree in catering. She calls me every year to wish me a happy birthday on April Fool's Day. What a 100-percent dear she is. Love you, Kate!

Not to get personal, but what size is your oven? Size matters, folks. Is it electric or gas? If gas, is it propane or natural gas? Is the propane tank full? Has the venue paid their gas bill? When was the last time it was cleaned? During Reagan's presidency? Be sure it works and check the temperature gauge for accuracy. Better yet, bring a laser thermometer and check it yourself. If you're used to reheating meals in your tiny little home kitchen oven at 375 degrees for twenty minutes, you have an entirely new experience in store for you with the full-sheet, commercial-sized convection ovens you'll encounter. If you or your caterer ruin the prepped food that had to have final cooking or reheating just before being served, then you're burnt toast! No es bueno. So, understand your venue's cooking landscape.

Reminder, NO ONE LIKES DRY-ASS CHICKEN.

I never use a microwave and most definitely don't want my food cooked or heated in one. But you should inquire to see if your event space uses one and check it out. What size is it? Is there more than one? Your full-sized platters won't fit in a dorm-sized micro. And when you have a lot of food to reheat, the first batch will end up cold (and rubbery) while you're waiting for the rest of the food to reheat. Plus, many catered food items come on metal trays and pans. You should know how well that works out (not) inside a microwave. I'd strongly suggest skipping the 'wave altogether. Paying for an excellent professional catering company is often worth it. #YouGetWhatYouPayFor.

Be sure to check out the coffee makers. How about coffee filters and spoons? Is there unlimited hot water for cooking? Did you remember to bring tea, along with honey and sweeteners? Did you inspect the prep tables? Is there a surface for your caterer to put things on? Think about the size of the area you need to prep and make sandwiches. Are the surfaces clean? The NOVA Way takes pride in keeping everything super clean. Thanks to superstars like James Greenwalt, Shawn Small, and Craig Dobbs, the team keeps our NOVA 535 venue super-duper clean. Clients and prospects notice anything that is not white-glove clean. #ExtraClean.

Think about garbage cans. You're going to need a bunch of them with liners. Does the can's appearance pass the "it'll be okay if guests see them" test? How badly do the garbage cans smell? The after-presence of stale beer and cigarettes, mixed with who-knows-what sticky substances, is enough to ruin the smell of any room—along with the attitudes and appetites of your special guests. Make sure someone hand-scrubs all the garbage cans before event night.

Carefully check the venue's back-of-the-house sinks. Are they three-compartment sinks? Hand sinks? Will your dirty dishes fit? Things, of course, will need to be rinsed off and washed properly, including your hands. Are the sinks dirtier than your hands? What is the team using to dry their hands and trays? Hopefully, they're not using their shirts and dresses. Be sure hand soap and dish soap are available. Is it all-natural or full of chemicals? Provide for ample supplies of serving trays, platters, tongs (not thongs, unless it's that kind of party), and utensils. Are you supplying them or is that your caterer's job? If they're provided on-site, do you like the looks of them? Do they match or clash with your theme? Are they polished clean, or is yesterday's (and last month's) gunk still stuck all over them?

Confirm your team has free and exclusive access to and from the kitchen. And that the kitchen will be properly cleaned before your caterer arrives. How are your caterers going to be loading in and out? Are they going to be walking past guests inside the party areas of the venue—which is beyond annoying to guests—or can they conveniently load in and out discreetly? At NOVA 535, we have alley access to our catering kitchen, so food vendors load in and out easily and get set up to feed everyone without disturbing guests. Remember, guests (mostly) all work for a living. They don't need to be reminded of work, cooking, cleaning, home, or—shoot, did they turn their oven off? They are at your event to relax, let off some steam, and enjoy themselves.

Kitchens are often staffed with day laborers, many of whom don't speak English. They are typically hard workers and may not be knowledgeable about your venue, expectations, language, or customs. The catering employees (locals) are often just trying to get through their shift or waiting for management to get out of sight so they can duck around back to post something on their latest blah-blah social sites or hit their vape. If they are wandering about and a guest asks them for directions to the restroom or for a glass of water, and their reply (which I see all over the globe) is a blank, uncomprehending stare, then your guests will be as disappointed as I've been.

A final note about commercial dishwashing equipment. This durable equipment goes a long way towards helping get all your dinner, flatware, and serving wares clean and ready to take home when the curtain closes on another long, challenging day. Make sure your venue has one, or possibly two commercial units (NOVA has two) and that they are clean and in good working order. Check the temp gauge, run them for a cycle, and inspect the freshly washed items for cleanliness. Commercial unit washing cycles run for just a few minutes, unlike the ones at home that can take an hour or more. After owning several commercial ones, I'm baffled as to why (aside from price) anyone would ever buy a home-style dishwasher again.

Chapter 9

Building Your Vendor Team

Food

Your selection of a catering (food service) company shouldn't be based on the lowest price. Price should come after quality and value. Do you remember the adage, "You get what you pay for?" Your focus should be on issues such as the number and type of catering staff assigned for your event.

Do you want day laborers or professionally trained servers and busboys? Do you want a soup chef (not even a sous-chef) or a "real" chef for your guests? Confirm that your caterer is providing an experienced team with a qualified captain/event manager. Make sure everything is written down. If you're super detail-oriented, ask for photos and resumes of team leaders to compare the day of. There is often a big difference between your vendor's A-team that was promised and the B-team that actually shows up—trust me. I've experienced "the great drop off."

Quality is improved by having well-rested, professionally trained servers who have pleasing personalities, compared to servers that were dropped off in a van by a temp-labor company. Trust me, staffing from labor pools is part of the hospitality landscape. When these bodies show up, you are lucky if they communicate in any language understandable anywhere on the planet. You quickly learn that you must tell them exactly what to do and then cross your fingers that they do the simplest tasks you ask of them. I have been reduced on some occasions to hoping a temp-laborer just stays out of the way during events. Don't be surprised to find servers and busboys on perpetual smoke breaks beginning the moment you turn your back. You can find yourself hoping that they haven't been searching for the bride's gift cards when no one was watching.

These risks call up the disadvantages of not knowing your vendors well, because things do go missing. Be careful to ensure that gifts and gift cards are locked up and secure. I've found that a trusted adult family member, chosen in advance, in charge of the gift card box, is the best plan. Add to that a decorative gift card box that is securely locked. When you have 150 guests and 40 vendors, that's 190 opportunities for someone to snatch something. The good news is, of course, most people you hire are good people and won't take advantage of you or heist things that don't belong to them.

When guests bring guests, they also bring additional risks. Remember our conversation about the ole plus-one? We use the same vendors most of the time, but vendors hire and fire people, and even good people go through bad times. The point is, you have to lock things up and assign someone you truly trust to protect against loss. It's best if someone from the client's side is protecting the valuables. Then the liability "ball" is in their court. We had an unfortunate incident years ago, and as a result, I added one of those hidden, "set your own combo" safes in our Supernova Suite the next week. Plus, we discuss and confirm with the client that they (not NOVA) have control of the gift card box. Now, if the client's Uncle Joe brings a nice check or a stack of Ben Franklins (one can only hope, right?), you have a plan and a discrete, locked location for the gifts. You've also agreed in advance that your client assumes all the oversight responsibility. They will be grateful that you're being thorough.

Buffets

There are two basic types of buffets. One is the guest self-serve buffet, and the other is a chef-attended buffet. Guest self-serve buffets are pretty self-explanatory. Guests approach the buffet line and serve themselves. In chef-attended buffets, as you might expect, a buffet-line "chef" elegantly (or shakily, haha) places food selections onto guests' plates.

Chef-attended buffets are themselves broken down into two subgroups. One offers ready-to-eat options, and the other has the chef cooking your selections to order. Chef-attended ready-to-eat buffets provide food that is (wait for it) ready to eat. Your guests point at or request some of this and some of that from the buffet, and the chef on duty (hopefully with elegance) helps the chosen food find its way onto your guests' plates.

For a cooked-to-order buffet, the chef offers custom ingredients and prepares dishes to order as directed by guests. Imagine the omelet station at your favorite fancy hotel. Keep in mind that it sounds fantastic to offer custom chef-cooked options—like a pasta station (yummy). But orders can take one to four minutes each, and with a hundred-plus guests, my back-of-the-napkin math adds up to four hundred minutes, or almost seven hours. This doesn't work for a quick-turnaround dinner schedule, absent a huge team of pro chefs on duty.

A brief word about chefs. Unless you budget accordingly, the chef attendants are actually cooks, not really chefs. Cooks take ingredients, like a nice pasta, and warm everything up in a skillet. A true chef is an entirely different animal. I've been fortunate enough to work with some of the best. Need a great one? Check out my chef pals like adventure chef Brent Shaver or Jason Ruhe, Chef Tony, Ted Dorsey, Jason Cline, Vegan Soul Chef Ray Milton, Murray Clements, Mickey Paleologos, Chef Chris Ponte, Colleen Travers, Ken Jurgensen, and, of course, my Momma! Bon appetito!

Take care when arranging tables for a buffet, because they are usually six or eight-foot-long rectangular tables, hopefully covered to the floor with linens. Plan for plenty of properly sized, un-wrinkled, clean linens. If your guests serve themselves, via the guest self-serve buffet, the table can be positioned along a wall. But for a chef-attended buffet table, you need three to five feet of space behind the table. This is so the chef(s) can easily get in and out to replenish the buffet with refreshed food and have ample working space to serve from.

A warning is appropriate here because occasionally, with chef-attended buffet stations, the chef will request additional space behind the station at the last minute. So, if you are starting with six to eight-foot-long rectangular tables, which are twenty-four to thirty inches wide, plus the three to five feet of space needed behind each chef for access, you still have to allow for space at the front of your serving (buffet) tables for guests to access their food. Your well-designed floor plan can quickly be upended if your favorite (or now not-so-favorite) chef decides at the last minute that there needs to be another table for a special dish she's been working on. These special chef dishes are usually ones that are added to the menu (by your client or a family member trying to "surprise" you) without your prior knowledge or approval.

The addition of such unexpected menu items calls attention to the planning necessary for having your menu locked down at least two weeks before the day of the event. Sometimes even the loss of one or two feet of valuable floor space turns tragic. Trust me here. This has been the source of one of my worst day-of nightmares over the last decade.

Here's what can happen. The catering company rolls in and wants to change the entire catering floor plan—or worse, they just do it themselves when you or your manager isn't looking. Many times, I've wanted to gently place my foot against the side of someone's head in utter frustration. Good thing I switched from kickboxing to yoga. I'm more inclined to "down dog" now instead of unleashing a roundhouse.

This is important, so listen up. The last-minute addition of one more table behind the chef can seriously mess up your event. Walk through the space with the catering company, with the tables in place, and make sure the flow will be great for them and for your guests' dining experience. Draw up the tables, along with their dimensions, ahead of time. Then have the chef and catering company literally sign off on your catering floor plan drawing.

Grease smoke choking your guests and sticking to their clothes? Not what you want to have happen. Ever. Well, it happens. If someone wants a "burger station," for example, and the animal fat grease isn't handled properly, the smoke billows out everywhere, maybe even setting off your fire alarm. These "good ideas" must be planned and then executed properly, using clean equipment, the right location, ventilation, etc. The last thing you want is for 99 percent of your amazing event to go to total shit because everyone smells like burnt hamburger. Hopefully, you are starting to fully comprehend the number of details involved and the value of a top-notch venue/ planner guiding you and preventing you from hitting the rocks and crashing your event into the shoals of shitty reviews and straight onto disappointment island.

Electricity

Here's something most planners overlook: electrical outlets. Be extra careful and do an inventory count of the facility's electrical outlets to confirm that there is adequate power capacity. Wiring is inside the walls and out of sight, so bring a tester. The outlets we all take for granted are typically strung together like lights on a Christmas tree inside those walls. There may be up to six outlets on a single (15 or 20-amp) circuit. One or more of them could be non-working.

Who cares, right? Umm, well, in support of your catering and buffet tables, you almost always find bright lights and food-warming lamps. And those heat lamps typically sit next to, let's say, a skillet, with a fryer or two close-by and maybe even a little pizza oven. Don't be surprised to see a microwave alongside that, as well. The breaker—or worse, a fuse—can pop when these power-hungry appliances are plugged into a little 15 or 20-amp circuit. They are just waiting to trip the breaker and rob guests of power.

Being powerless in the middle of an event sucks. Everything stops, literally. Each of those appliances can draw 5 to 15 or more amps of power, and when you plug two, three, or four of them into a single chain of outlets, boom. There goes your 15-amp fuse/breaker. And possibly your hopes of hot food tonight.

The wiring in some venues is so old because the venues themselves are old. Luckily for NOVA 535 and our guests, and my experience of renovating over a hundred older homes and apartments, I appreciate the importance of electrical capacity. I hired Jim Walker, a five-star electrician, and added construction guru Michael Mitchell to teach me even more about where the wiring should go and how much power was needed. Also, hiring a world-class plumber, like Jon Aljasir, is critical because where there is water, you will need power. Plumbing and electrical work together like a fine duet.

We done real good at NOVA 535. It's funny—well, not really—that after (over) wiring everything, that's when Bluetooth and Wi-Fi were just becoming widely available.

When wiring becomes an issue the day of your event, you might be observed scrambling for extension cords.

Did you bring them? You were probably seen laying those ugly, trip-inducing orange ropes across the room to access the power supply. We've had clients who make last-minute changes or additions, but that info never makes it to the venue-planner, which means the floorplan wasn't adjusted to accommodate extra skillets, warmers, and fryers.

By the way, have you ever had fried doughnuts with ice cream on top? The idea is fantastic (except for all the sugar, gluten, preservatives, etc.), but, hey, clients love ordering that stuff. Unfortunately, the power demands go apeshit when things like this are included in the menu. Think about adding a skillet that draws 8 amps, let alone a 12-amp fryer. Where does the mini 10-amp ice cream freezer go that someone requested at the last minute? These create a huge power drain, which causes tripped breakers, which means you lose power here—and most likely elsewhere, probably at the DJ booth. You find yourself asking, "Where are the breakers to restore power?" Worse, if you discover that your venue is still using screw-in glass fuses and they've blown, that means your electricity (along with Elvis) has left the building. So, at that point, you can grab a bottle and start drinking.

With our newly engineered power service at NOVA, we have plenty of power at every event. Whenever you're at a lesser venue or one that is scheduled outdoors, etc., the failure to confirm power supply can lead to real problems. Think it through in advance. Do not *ass*-u-me.

We prioritize planning, and that's just one of the many reasons major film and TV production companies like *60 Minutes*, *Dateline*, and regional powerhouses like Red Lizard Films, Scatter Brothers, and Diamond View Studios book their events with NOVA. They bring film and TV industry influencers like Jonni Watts, Commissioner Tony Armer,

Curtis Graham, Elizabeth Overcast, Michael Baumgarten, Mildred Mattos, Rose Rosen, and fitness gurus Tony Little and Forbes Riley, who love shooting at our site. We've got all the clean power they need. Shooting is way too expensive to worry about tripped breakers. At NOVA, it's lights, camera, and plenty of action.

Buffet Line Engineering

Planning for the cooked-to-order buffet line, with its pasta and or other creation stations, needs to be carefully done. Why? The idea of a pasta station manned by an on-duty chef who custom-makes delicious, fresh pasta for your guests sounds fantastic, no? Yes, of course, it does. Here's the rub. When guests—especially very hungry guests who may also be a little buzzed from glasses of vino or whatever—begin smelling the irresistible aroma of fresh pasta smothered in veggies, meats, and cheesy sauces, they are going to queue up and want some of that delicious food. Like, now.

So, let's say your chef station is running perfectly. (This almost never happens, because you're dealing with humans, but let's pretend.) And let's say your guests are super intelligent and fast decision makers. They make their way through the buffet line snatching up food items lickety-split. They seem focused on putting in their orders with military-quick time. (Haha! Not a chance. But remember, we're pretending.) The best-case outcome is for each individual order to be placed, the fresh hot pasta cooked and then served in one minute. (Best case. A reality check puts it at two to three minutes. But let's pretend one minute.)

Let's see, now. . . . There were how many guests? Probably 100. That means 100 guests times one minute to serve each guest, as the best case in a perfect-world scenario.

That means you have a 100-minute buffet line. Of course, not everyone will want pasta. And, of course, they won't each order and receive it in one minute, so on average, a minute per guest is still optimistic. At my brother Chris' NOVA 535 wedding, we had 150 guests and hired four pasta chefs. We didn't want people waiting up to an hour and a half for their pasta, and because of our planning, they didn't have to.

Dinners are typically scheduled to last forty-five to ninety minutes. It's really important to think about the big picture of your serving line process. Then you can produce a nice dinner flow for guests. Buffet dinners are great for many reasons, and when done properly, they give guests a chance to come to the food selection tables, choose a delicious, custom plate of food for dinner, enjoy those moments of being "in charge" of the chef, mingle with each other, and spend time exploring the venue—all the while making new friends. Just make sure that you've planned the best station locations for both the guest self-serve and chef-attended models.

Plan the menu and presentation professionally to delight your guests. Have large font and easy-to-read item menus. People are increasingly picky about what they eat, and Ms. Fussy Pants will hold up the entire line to confirm whether this is goat or sheep cheese. Accurately and completely label everything. Use universal symbols; VN = vegetarian, V = vegan, GF = gluten free.

Find the perfect balance between guest satisfaction and keeping things on schedule. How? Hire a 5-Star catering company. NOVA has been thrilled to work with Adventure Chef Brent Shaver, Puff and Stuff, Elite Events Catering, Murray's, The Mill DTSP, Delectables, Olympia, Chives, Ray's Vegan Soul, Mickey's Organics, Mise en Place, Cafe Ponte, In Bloom, Catering by the Family, Banyan and St. Pete Taco Lady Colleen Travers, to name a few.

IT'S 5 AM GO HOME

Yeah, I'm name-dropping, so what? The time has come to make a food baby.

Buffet Line Scheduling

Whenever food is being prepared, it's important to stick to your event schedule the day of, because when the food is hot and ready to serve, every minute waiting in cooldown mode eso no es bueno. You can wiggle around just about any other part of your event schedule. It doesn't matter too much if the speeches, dances, or short videos are off-schedule a bit, but not so when it comes to your guests' food. You want to be thinking Swiss train schedules, which, as we know, are always on time. Who raves about cold, dry chicken? No one does. But who is pissed about it? Everyone. Protect your food schedule like a newborn infant. Everything else works around it.

Plated to the Table

The "plated" food serving model uses servers to bring pre-selected dinners on plates directly to guests seated at their tables. Unless there are guest name cards (seating cards), guests seat themselves anywhere at their designated tables, which can make connecting the right meal with the right person a challenge, unless everyone at a table is selecting the same exact thing from your menu (haha, not). Of course, the waiter could scream out, "Where's the beef?" but this isn't the corner deli. So, a "plated" model invites some chaos and disorder. A seasoned (food pun) pro waiter could discreetly ask each guest, "Chicken or fish, ma'am?" There are advantages and disadvantages to this, a smaller guest count makes this option more flexible and less work, and it allows you to skip the seating cards, which require significant effort.

The table setting card option assigns guests to a specific seat at a specific table. Table seating cards indicate that Ms. Alexis Smith is in Seat #3 at Table #6. Each assigned seat has a preordered menu item prepared and delivered to the guest in that seat. It's lots of work for everyone. I strongly advise against assigning individual seats for guests. Better instead to just assign people to specific tables. Then those people can choose whatever seat they want and decide who they want to sit next to. Much less work with virtually the same results. The guest can acquire their seating card, typically found on a table or such. During the cocktail hour is a perfect time. Then they just place their menu card on their dinner plate so the waitstaff can then set down the appropriate meal.

Family Style

Family style is an option where the server brings huge bowls of food for everyone at a table. When servers arrive, they ask each seated guest, "Would you like some ____?" There is a variation on this model, which works as long as your table is large enough; you can leave self-serving bowls filled and replenished (by the waitstaff) at each table and allow each table's guests to serve themselves. This can also be done with wine. The server leaves a bottle of red and white wine at each table, chosen by the host or caterer, which has wine glasses in place for each diner, so people who drink wine can serve themselves. It's like having dinner with your family at your parent's dining room table. Hence the name "family style." There may be less bickering than at home, but that depends on who you're inviting to your event.

Back in 1987, my father, Michael Francis Novilla, took my brother Chris and me to explore Italy. By random chance, our good friend Luis Garcia was also "invited" along. Lou was serving in the US Army and stationed in northern Italy, which was close to where the tour started. Lou joined us for about two weeks. Basically, we snuck him along with us as we embarked. The package included food, drinks, transportation, and lodging. Lou is smooth with the ladies and charmed our bella tour guide Anna, where everything went spingere, piano, bravo.

By the time we made it to Venice, Anna had fallen in love with Lou (of course she did), so we got to share in their royal "romance." We had a magnificent five-hour, ten-course dinner, all family style. It was one of the most amazing meals I've ever had. The waitstaff kept returning to our tables, offering endless courses of ensalada, pasta, carne, and frutta di mare. I often wish I could say thanks again to Dad, who was such a wonderful guy and always took great care of everyone.

Family style was "Noviello" style, prior to Ellis Island, when Noviello was changed to Novilla. Yet that is a novella for another tempo!

Butler-Passed Hors D'oeuvres

Butler-passed hors d'oeuvres, are appetizers passed around during your event. This is a great addition to your guests' dining experience and is most always used at the early part of events. It encourages guests to mingle, talk, network, schmooze, or whatever while servers greet them with a delicious taste of some (fill in the blank). This is great for guests during the notorious cocktail hour, which may or may not actually last an hour—typically forty-five to ninety minutes. Many modern brides don't want their guests sitting too much, or even at all, during their weddings. So, butler-passed munchies accommodate the bride's wishes. It's also a great way to welcome people as they arrive for your event and take the edge off an aggressive appetite. It's a nice surprise and sets up anticipation for, "Oh, what's next?"

Butler-passed works especially well when there isn't a lot of room for food to be displayed, and it's appropriate when your food budget barely meets the number of guests in attendance. Remember, people tend to pig out when they are at the buffet. Yes, people like you. We all tend to overload our plates. So, passing small samples in quantities that you, the host, or caterer controls is an important management tool to make the event more financially palatable (another food pun). The alternative is to let people pile their plates sky-high from the buffet line and monitor their disappointment when the "good stuff" runs out.

Food Trucks

Have you considered bringing in a food truck or two? Food trucks are modern, fun, and save quite a bit of money off your final invoice. If you use them, plan for how guests are going to get their food from the truck to their tables.

Important questions: Who cleans up the tables afterwards? Also, what are you providing your guests to eat their food *on*? Are you supplying single-use plates? Please make sure everything is eco-friendly. Have you considered renting china with the idea of stationing it near the trucks? That's something you should discuss with truck vendors. They typically have their own preference to help expedite their orders, so make sure to discuss details with them well in advance. And what do we do with all details and expectations? Repeat after me. "We get them in writing, Michael. Signed by both parties."

There is much to consider with a food truck option. What will you do if it rains or if a cold snap suddenly swoops in from the wintry north? What if the truck has to park too far away? What side of the truck is the food served from? Then also consider the timing and length of your guests' dining experience. Remember, one of your guests has a grandmother with a bad knee. How is she going to be served from a food truck? You may need to consider hiring an extra server or two to assist with mobility-challenged guests. There needs to be a comprehensive plan that accommodates those who aren't so mobile.

What is the scenery around the truck? Dumpsters? A sexy (not) parking lot? That will be a part of your guests' dining experience that they remember. Is the area secure? At NOVA 535, we accommodate three food trucks easily inside our private, secure, and gorgeous brick and bamboo courtyard. The food's ready. Let's eat.

The quality of the truck itself is critical. It must be clean and quiet. It must have a generator—and not some version of a loud, smelly headache-inducing old generator with diesel fumes galore, which instantly ruins your guests' happiness. Friends like Colleen Travers, aka the St. Pete Taco Lady, and Maggie "On the Move" Loftin offer delicious, fresh food with clean, modern, quiet trucks as a feature of their services. They are such lovely, hardworking (and fun) ladies. Bottom line, food trucks can be a fantastic catering solution, yet, as always, do your homework and do not *ass*-u-me that all will be okay without written details and close supervision.

Beverages and the Bar

Ask yourself, "What type of party is this?" Are you planning a kids' carnival? Are you hosting a wedding? Is it a corporate product launch? What's the size of your budget? Regardless of the category, beverages will be a significant part of your event budget, and so nowadays, many events offer a blend of prepaid and guest self-pay cash/credit at the bar for drinks. Prepaid bars by the event host are also known as "open" or "hosted" bars where the client/host prepays for guest drinks, for a set amount of time, which (hopefully, from the guests' POV) is for the entire event.

A subcategory of the prepaid bar is the "consumption" bar, with other terms used in other parts of the world to describe this option. This is where the host hands over her credit card, and the bar runs a tab for either a preset time or amount or even an unlimited tab. At the end of the event, that tab is settled between the client and the bar manager. This can be really smart when your attendance is unknown, as prepaying for two hundred guests—and that is nonrefundable—versus a consumption tab set at $2500, limits your risk. You, the host, can always expand that tab during the event as the guest count grows.

Then there is a cash bar, where the bartenders—hopefully, but not always, so confirm in advance—accept cash and credit cards so that guests can purchase their own drinks at the bar.

Let's look at the two different types of bars, and who pays what, so there is no confusion.

Paid by Guests = Cash Bar

This is simple. Your guests go up to the bar, order a drink, and pay for it with cash or credit card. Hence, the term "cash bar."

Paid by Event Host = Prepaid Bar, Open Bar, Hosted Bar, or Consumption Bar

Oh, your lucky guests. Someone—the host, their grandma, or a rich uncle Joe—has picked up the tab for drinks. This can be for some or all of the event. What drinks, specifically, is an important question. Here at NOVA 535, we offer several different packages.

Coffee, Tea, and Lemonade
Juice and Soda
Beer and Wine
House, Call, Premium, and Supernova Liquor Packages.

All our beverage packages include items from the lower tier. So, our Premium Liquor Package, for example, includes call liquors, beer and wine, and juice and soda, plus the coffee, tea, and lemonade package offerings.

What about mixers? Your soda package could include the following; Coke, Diet Coke, Sprite, ginger ale, sour mix, and water. Water should be filtered and offered as a tonic, soda, and just plain H2O. Don't forget the frozen version of water: ice. NOVA offers juices including orange, pineapple, cranberry, grapefruit, and tomato (Bloody Marys, anyone?) as our standbys. NOVA's standard condiments include lemons, limes, olives, and cherries.

There is always a tradeoff between offering "what people want," like Diet Coke, and what is good for them. Drinking diet anything is not good for you. Always read the label.

You could go nutso in the condiment space. Should you include oranges, fresh mint, seasonal berries (blueberries, blackberries, strawberries, you get it) and so on? Early in my career, I remember promising a client a seasonal berry mixer. I totally forgot that those particular berries were not in season on the wedding date. Dopey me, I had to scramble and find new sources to keep the promise. Thinking back, as it turned out, I don't think her guests ended up requesting any of those berries in specialty cocktails, anyway. So, guess which venue owner enjoyed an expensive fruit shake as their shift drink? Their name rhymes with bike. But kept promises verses broken promises (and matched or mismatched expectations) are what make or break a business.

Specialty Cocktails

Specialty cocktails can either be an excellent idea or a terrible idea, depending on the event. My web development guru, close friend, and mastermind, Chris Jenkins, often admonishes me, "Michael, that's a terrible idea!" He's saved me from self-inflicted disasters many times. It's no wonder he and his amazing superwoman wife, Kym Jenkins, always drink free at my bar. By this point in our lives, we have both become professional drinkers and know exactly what we want. Younger clients and event planners, however, can get all bubbly and excited about offering specialty cocktails.

The key thing to remember about specialty cocktails is to be sure that they are quick and easy for your bartender to make. They can be a fun way to introduce newer drinkers—which is to say, younger drinkers—to cocktail-land. These younger, less experienced drinking clients can get all starry-eyed when making decisions on their specialty drink preferences. I've seen them go crazy over seasonal berries and at least seventeen other weird ingredients. They are not concerned, of course, that each cocktail takes six minutes to make. So, we do our best to talk those guests with fresher livers out of their predisposition for ordering strange, complex drinks. We want them to choose specialty drinks that are fun to say, pretty to see, easy to make, and delicious to drink. That's where we want to be.

Why? Well, for a corporate event or a wedding, people can arrive in waves. It's nothing like a restaurant or bar, which fills up gradually. Typically, people at events come in waves and almost always at announced times. I've bartended plenty, and although I'm not a pro, I'm pretty good when it comes to making drinks. But remembering the ingredients for a few oddball concoctions snags me up occasionally. I dread seeing that look of impatience and despair on clients' faces when I ask our real bartenders, "Tell me, what's in this drink again?" For example, if someone orders a Long Island Iced Tea, I roll my eyes for so many reasons.

If you are behind the bar at a wedding or event with one hundred and fifty guests, you have to be well prepped and ready when they suddenly descend on you like a swarm of thirsty frat boys. Unlike a bar or restaurant that fills up gradually, you can get waves of twenty-five, fifty, and even one hundred and fifty people coming at you—the bartender—all at once. Think cocktail hour in a stampede. So, with one hundred, one hundred and fifty, two hundred, or, shit, two hundred and fifty guests descending upon your three, four, or, at most, five bartenders, that's a hoard of thirsty peeps. Here at NOVA 535, our math is typical for the industry; one bartender for every seventy-five guests. You will need three or maybe four bartenders for an event with two hundred guests, all of whom are ready to drink. Always ask your client to guess the drinking level of their guests. Often, brides and grooms know the guests who will be ready to party. So, adding an extra bartender for a few hundred bucks, if that reduces an agonizing wait at the bar, is money well spent!

Every tiny delay leads to frowns and frustrations. It's not unusual for people to feel uncomfortable in new places, in large groups, or especially when dolled up for your big event. Picture them in a rental tux or uncomfortable new stilettos (you go, girl!) and remember that they've already spent time circling the block because the host didn't think to spend the extra money for valet parking. Parking is still a hassle. So, listen. Your guests can be a bit uptight and possibly a tad sweaty, and they are jostling in line for their first drink to take the edge off. Make sure if you are doing specialty cocktails, that they are easy-peasy to make. Drinking = smiling. Waiting = frowning. If those specialty drinks take forever and a day to make, with mulling and super-specialized ingredients flown in from Bavaria that must be hand-peeled, people can—no, will—get pissy-faced. And that is not how you want to start your event.

Let's review. Fun to say, pretty to see, easy to make, and delicious to drink. That's where we want to be! Cheers!

Doorman and Security

Is there a difference between a doorman and security? The short and long answer is, yes. One has surgical precision, and the other is a blunt instrument.

Your doorman is someone who greets guests on their way in with a warm, smiling face and welcoming eyes. "Welcome to NOVA. Please come straight in; your entry is up and to your left. Have a wonderful evening, folks." He/she scans the streets and occupants for signs of trouble. Then, as the event is ending and your guests exit, the doorman offers this: "Thanks for joining us at NOVA tonight. I hope you all had a wonderful time. Do you have your keys, phone, etc.? Oh, and I'll take that, please," (the cocktail or bottle of cerveza in the wobbly guest's hands). Your doorman also helps manage guests that should not be driving, and helps with rideshare/taxis, etc.

The doorman is your welcome and goodbye to guests and also your first and last line of defense. They are friendly, but not too much. They never blab with guests or hold up the line, and you screen to avoid hiring that lonely, creepy dude as a doorman—a guy who wants to chat everyone up. They are polite, welcoming, always wearing a smile, and eternally vigilant. They dress nice and smell of nothing. They're not on their phone and not eating nor chewing gum. You're paying your doorman to observe everything. They watch carefully for an unwanted and uninvited guest who might be somebody's ex in stalker mode. It might be a poor homeless guy hoping to saunter in and enjoy some high-class buffet. Who can blame him? Your doorman is watching for those random, loud, hammered dudes who just happen to be strolling down from the sports bar nearby. Or someone like me who is traveling solo and has sniffed out a great party from miles away—the guy who hears just the right vibes and senses this is the perfect party to crash. Which I have done in many countries and many types of events, ably breaching their security many times. Except in Kyoto.

Did I mention Japan? It was my birthday, and I tried to access an ultra-private, Japanese members-only lounge. It was the holy grail of that city during that time. I failed, though, only after getting a respectful, knowing smirk from the Yakuza doormen. I replied to their "Japanese members only" with, "But I am Japanese!" Kanpai!

Your doorman's most critical role is being your front door filter. That door needs to open only when welcoming your guests but closed and secure at all other times. Certainly, a doorman can either be a doorman or a doorwoman, since both sexes just as easily fill this role. The thing is, I haven't seen it equalize that much yet. I have already decided to accept the obvious: Women are more perceptive than guys. Anyway, your door-person needs to be chosen carefully, and you must have confidence that he or she can handle things professionally and effectively when, not if, things go sideways.

If a guest gets touchy or if there is an altercation or something else out of the ordinary happens, the doorman/door-person needs to be able to use physical force to protect your guests and the venue. They really must have professional training and skills. You don't want a security monster here looking to smash someone onto the sidewalk, since that will lead to lawsuits and ER room visits; lose-lose. You want a smooth takedown but as a last resort. It should be done quietly, efficiently, and safely, without bothering you or your guests. Think about perfect weather = perfect customer service = everything is done just right, so you and your guests never even notice.

There are many things that should be planned behind the scenes for your event and party that your guests don't need to know anything about (kinda like real life). When guests are going out with the expectation to party, they want to leave the stress, kids, work, politics, headaches, and worries behind them so they can maximize their enjoyment of your event. I call it "the bubble," and I compare it to visiting Disney World.

In fact, when we designed NOVA 535, I made sure that our glass windows and doors were opaque, so once our guests were inside, they could only see, hear, and interact with those sights, sounds, and smells that have been prepared for their enjoyment inside the venue. We don't want anything to pop their bubble. Once they are at our party or event, we don't want them to see or even think about the parking lot, the traffic, the noise, or the mess and stresses of the world outside. We only want them to relax and enjoy themselves.

Your security, as opposed to your doorman, are typically those massive walls of muscled flesh that wear the bright red or yellow "security" shirts pulled taut over their bulging frames. They are there to (not so) subtly showcase that there are consequences for breaking the rules and that the host has a backup.

Physical altercations—knock-down, drag-out, hair-pulling scraps and fights—do break out. And it often involves other beefcakes, although occasionally it can be the ladies. So, your security team has best be professionally trained and ready, willing, and able to get things back under control quickly and quietly. Think of a football linebacker trained with black belt skills and a samurai warrior's Zen calm. And patience, 'cause they will be tested.

Security needs to be ready to "dance" at a moment's notice and yet not be easily provoked. Security staff should screen out hotheads; calm and measured is the goal. They should be seen walking quietly and acting as the big stick. Hopefully, you'll never see them in action, but NOVA 535 considers them equivalent to having car insurance. You almost never need it until you do need it. Then you are glad you hired a high-quality, professionally licensed, and insured security company. Or you'll be pissed because you were cheap and went with an unprofessional security team.

Things can so south real fast when there are a lot of people in hot, tight quarters and testosterone is flowing! Once a fight starts, it can spiral quickly out of control. We've used Jason Nosal's Signature Security out of St. Pete for years, and they've always handled things like pros. Jason has since moved on to other opportunities—a fellow evolving Entrepreneur!

Valet

Your choice of valet is an important decision, same as with your doorman and security. It's super important that your valets are perceived by guests as friendly, warm, welcoming, responsible, and trustworthy. After all, guests are literally giving them the keys to their cars—literally handing someone their car and often their house keys. You want them to represent you well in their interactions with your guests, especially toward the EON, as guests can get a little buzzed, tired, horny, whatever, and, at such times, forgetful and predisposed to driving home after having a bit too much to drink.

 If you drive a car, have a valet key ready for times like this. Handing any stranger your full set of house, office, and whatever else keys isn't smart.

Your valet should come from a well-respected, professionally trained, and of course, fully licensed and insured organization. We've used several over the years at NOVA 535. Our top pick is Courtesy Valet, run by my pal Shawn Downing, with help from his right-hand guys, Jeff and Kris. We have our valet and doorman/security remain at our events until all the guests have left. At that point, we do a sweep, which is a physical inspection of the property, to make sure no guests are left behind, lingering, or occasionally even passed out.

We once had a guest who went into the restroom and locked the door before he got sick and passed out. No one knew he was there until our EON process kicked in. During the sweep, we discovered that one of our ten restroom suits had a locked door. The only way to inspect the locked restroom was to pick the lock, and when we did, we found him on the floor, sleeping like a baby. Well, until we woke the poor dude up. It turned out he was one of our very talented local artists. He was barely old enough to drink legally and hadn't—like all of us at some point—gotten his personal drinking certification card yet.

All ended well, however, after a little embarrassment on his part. All of us have at some point have drunk too much and said or done something regretful. We may have even gotten sick or what-have-you. I am sure it was a learning experience, and he probably moved forward starting the next morning.

As I've mentioned elsewhere, I started experimenting with drinking and partying at age eleven, which was the time I also started my first lawn mowing company. I was a kid, sipping on some beers and occasionally smoking some weed. I hung with the older kids, and so goes the cycle of life. If there are classes that teach the art of drinking and partying, I'd be happy to guest lecture. The more you know, the smarter your decision making can be.

Your doorman and valet are key components for your EON procedures. When you throw several weddings and events every week like I do, you develop a well-planned and consistent EON process. Which brings me to the lost and found.

Everybody forgets things. Parties and events seem to be all about forgetting. The need to leave all the drama and BS from home, work, school, family, and whatever, calls up the desire to escape for a while. Unfortunately, personal items also love to escape from their owner's grasp. Things like keys, phones, purses, sweaters, jewelry, clothing (now that's a great party!) shoes (OMG!), wedding cakes, the groom (yes, seriously), etc.

As part of your EON process, even if you are hosting only one event, remember what your mother taught you about kids. They are all special. We love them and treat them with attention and respect. Otherwise, they'll run out in the streets. Think of event hosting the same way. Have a process in place. Expect things to be left behind. Find them before their owners head homeward. We've even created a NOVA 535.com/Lost (for our guests) making the recovery process easy for everyone.

EON Sweeps

Guys love to take off their jackets and ladies sometimes leave sweaters, purses, party gifts, phones (when dancing, for example) at their tables. Guests can be hanging in the back near the bar, making out on the balcony, or bumming smokes off vendors in the alley. People can and will forget about their personal possessions. So, for your own sanity the next day and to avoid frantic calls—or worse, people pounding on your door at 5:00 AM—have your staff, team, and possibly yourself, do a sweep of the property for anything guests may have unintentionally left before they leave.

Our rule at NOVA 535 is that everything must be accounted for during EON sweeps. Pretty much every vendor will test you on this, and it's best to be firm. It's like the tide at the beach. Everything comes in on the day of, and then everything must leave (go out) after the event ends. No exceptions. That includes chairs, tables, stages, boxes, gifts, cakes, food, newlyweds, etc.

The caterer's staff is responsible for bussing tables, so they are well-positioned to find missing car keys, phones, and the like. When the band or DJ is about two songs away from the final announcement of the "last song of the night," that's a good time to send your catering staff around to all the tables and look in every corner where guests have been hanging out to search for missing items. Have your team walk around holding up missing shoes or a purse they found, and ask everyone as they leave to double check for phones, keys, and possessions. Ask your team to look under tables, in restrooms, anywhere and everywhere people congregate—especially at the bar—with an eye out for anything that doesn't belong. Extra time and vigilance spent checking for lost items will more than make up for the annoyance of those next-day frantic texts and phone calls. Trust me.

Cleanup

Most parties tend to be scheduled for Friday and Saturday nights, and you can expect to pay extra for late-night and weekend pickup. But after more than 2,000 successful events, we always want our event rentals and vendor items taken home that same night. Have your cleaning crew finish up with a good cleaning and mopping. Using a floor steam cleaner is even better. Don't leave those spilled, disgusting, what-the-fuck-is-that liquids on your floors. Those sticky messes from undetermined origins don't smell any better and for sure aren't easier to clean twenty-four to forty-eight hours later.

Be a pro here. Put up the extra money and implement EON procedures so that everything gets cleaned and removed right away, and the next day, you'll awake to a fresh and clean space. It shouldn't be a choice. The alternative is a sticky, disgusting nightmare in the morning. People are tired at 1 AM to 5 AM. I suggest bringing in a fresh cleaning crew or even hiring additional cleaners if you have to, including college kids looking for extra spending money. Bring them in to collect trash.

Speaking of which, make sure you have extra garbage cans and properly sized bags (don't get cheap here) throughout the venue. Beer bottles and liquids are heavy; try lifting a case of beer. Torn bags with disgusting contents spewing all over your shoes, the flooring, and wherever else is not helpful or good for your mood at the end of a long, long night.

Have your cleaning team arrive, say, thirty to sixty minutes before your event is scheduled to end. Let them come in to augment the on-duty crew who may have snuck in some drinks, smokeries, etc, during the event. Now, to be clear, that is 100 percent a no-no. During work time, the team needs to be fresh and sober, focused on work. It needs to be clear to all crew members that there is no downing shots with guests, and no sneaking into the alley to get a quick drag off a cig or a blunt. In Florida, which is a right to work state, you don't have to offer smoke breaks. Smoking cigarettes causes all kinds of cancer and doesn't leave your mouth all smoochy fresh, in case you are new to planet Earth.

Think about this for a second. Smoking cigarettes is a known killer. It has zero redeeming qualities, aside from the relaxing buzz of nicotine. But balancing that with the hundreds of known carcinogens? Bottom line, smoking is disgusting! Bottom line, smoke breaks are unhealthy and a waste of time that tends to feed a drug habit. So, NOVA doesn't allow our crews to stop work, go harm themselves, stink up their breath and clothing, and then come back into the venue around our valued guests.

Our crew rules prohibit gum chewing and personal odors resembling anything except fresh and clean. No body sprays or perfumes, because those are poisons going into your body. Smell is one of the human body's oldest and most powerful senses. What our team members may personally enjoy, our guests may hate. Combining perfume and gum with cigarette smells is a no bueno.

So, this circumlocution—I love that word—has a point. Which is, your team and staff should not appear untrained or as if they don't give a shit. If they appear to be partaking and sloppy at the end of your event (the end of an eight to twelve-hour day), that's when mistakes happen. Without professional management, they *will* happen. That's when cleaning gets ignored, monies get miscounted, accidents happen, final invoices and bar tab payments are not collected, and so on. It's a sloppy time.

The event business can be like the military in some respects. (Though to be clear, I've never served and am thankful to those who have. We humans should dedicate ourselves to more parties and less war.) Even planning is like the military in that it has clearly defined roles and duties, a hierarchy, with a commander. NOVA's systems and routines are our friends. Especially when there are 5 parties this week, and we're 11 hours deep into number 4. We provide an EON list that is conveniently on every crew member's phone, which they are not supposed to be using for texting or playing games during the event. Our MyNovaEvent.com system provides all our team members and vendors with event info, including their EON list. Today's crack is digital notifications, so good luck trying to keep people off their phones. Except when they are supposed to be following the EON list. Good luck dealing with this.

The boot camp saying is, "If you have time to lean (against the wall), then you have time to clean." Using that military analogy, think of a ship. Or even better, a yacht. I was so fortunate to spend lots of time on boats and ships, usually with the Puglieses and Nicklauses. I learned that everything has a place, is well-maintained and kept polished sparkling clean.

I'll always remember my friend who married a billionaire and took us around Sicily for a few weeks in their over 204 foot mega yacht. Talk about clean and everything in its place! That was an extraordinary example of 10-Star service. That's how a venue should be arranged. It's good for inventory, as vendors unintentionally, and occasionally intentionally, walk away with your stuff. If you have a shelf for coffee carafes and there are supposed to be fifteen of them stored there, it's easy for everyone to know where they belong. Everyone I know can count to quince.

Using the Spanish word for fifteen, quince, reminds me of my trips to South America. I'm fortunate to have been to almost all of North and South America and a few countries in Central America as well. The fellow Americans I met there are lovely people, and, surprise, most all of them speak Spanish. Many come to the United States to find a better life. My own great-grandparents originated from England, Scotland, Ireland, Czechoslovakia, and Italy. Wherever people are from, our country (should) invite honest, good people who want to work hard and share the American dream: making a better life for themselves.

Our American immigration system is clearly broken, so much so that I was unable to (successfully) invite my girlfriend Huyen from Vietnam to visit. Her passport falls into the (virtually automatic) "VISA DENIED" category. No real reasons given. So, think about that; I'm a well-respected, native-born American citizen with no felonies, the holder of a valid driver's license, voter ID, and passport, an MBA from the University of South Florida, and a successful small business owner, yet I cannot invite my friend from Vietnam to visit me at my home in Florida. *WTF?*

Back to the business at hand. EON processes. With a well run machine, everyone has a role and a process to follow. There are established places for your inventory—places you can point to and show people who may not speak English so they can understand. Trust me. I'm trying to learn a second language, now and es difícil. Despite traveling throughout most of their delightful countries and loving their cultures, I'm still struggling with languages. Mi Espanol es poco muy malo. I've been through Spain itself, as well as Colombia, Perú, México, Puerto Rico, Panamá, Costa Rica, Ecuador, Chile, Argentina, Paraguay, Uruguay, East LA (haha!), and Brazil. Well, if you're paying attention, you know that Brazilians speak Portuguese. There's just enough Espanol mixed into Portuguese to make me sound more like a payaso (clown)! I gave up and switched to Google Translate, throwing in as mucho obrigado as possible!

The point is that if your inventory is well thought-out and organized, you can easily point to where things go, no hablar necessary. Showing someone where the garbage bags are or where to find wine glasses can be done without speaking.

Having just visited Brazil during the summer of 2017 (Foz, São Paulo, and Rio) after about three weeks, I found their Portuguese language, a combination of English, Spanish, and Italian, to be a very sexy language, yet extremely difficult and dangerous to get careless with. Just when you think you can speak some Portuguese, be careful—ter cuidado. They have many similar words with very different meanings. When you are trying to say, "I want to tip you," you may be calling the waitress a prostitute, which can make for an interesting scenario—one you might either enjoy, or, much more likely, one where her seventeen cousins are beating the blanco out of you in the alley behind her restaurant. No mas, por favor!

If you make your crew's rules clear and simple, and enforce them, you will have created a well-run, military-style machine. Crew members show up for work clean, sober, smelling of nothing, no gum-chewing and bright-eyed, with cell phones and purses put away and no smoking or drugging—never until work is 100 percent completed. Plus, each team member clearly understands his or her role, tasks and duties.

The event world is all about people serving people. As we slip into our collective future, technology will continue to enhance our lives with smarter phones, blockchains, etc., while also eliminating certain jobs. I am thinking of things like driving, bartending, sex robots (you look it up!), and so on, leaving us with a whiff of uncertainty. Of course, all of that is a great reason to throw a party. Until then, make sure that all your vendors and team know their exact roles and expectations. Leave no room for any confusion. Neither bartenders nor vendors are ever allowed to drink alcohol or get high on duty, period.

Feeding Your Vendors

Feeding your vendors is a requirement. Timing is part of that process. The photographer and DJ need to schedule the best time for them to eat. The entire staff needs to be fed and well hydrated, all night. Make sure you include vendor meals and have taken time to discuss them with your caterer and, of course, your paying client.

Also, discuss the timing of the meals and where they are going to happen. Are they eaten in the kitchen? No! Where they can be seen by guests? No! Take a few smart moments and plan this out. You will thank me later.

Chapter 10

Planning

Decor

It's those little—and sometimes not so little—touches that make your party uniquely special. I realized that during our setup for Dr. Dan Hameroff's fortieth birthday party back in 2008. Mom, Helen, decorated the tables, and in about sixty minutes, she transformed the dining tables from plain linen to wowzers. I was a real estate guy, not an event decorator. Seeing a real pro like her in action made me realize I needed to step up my game, big time.

Helen, who I call my fairy godmother, also introduced me to her pals, including superstar event guru Phyllis Eig. Both ladies contributed love kindness and wisdom into our growing NOVA-verse. Love and hugs to them both.

One of those little decorating touches I love is candles. They seem to have a primordial energy and hypnotic allure that draws guests to their open flame. I've had our guests tell me that our candles at NOVA remind them of gulf beach sunsets, oceans, and those things we find in nature that have a uniquely powerful yet calming flow of energy.

When guests are seated at their tables, be sure to have candles of some sort and maybe a centerpiece. Keep in mind that centerpieces and candles can be magnificent, yet they can end up consuming too much of the table's real estate and can block guests' views of each other and everything else going on. Think about your wedding's first dance. Don't you want that to be visible without your guests having to stand up? Select a size and shape for an appropriate centerpiece. With that, plus candles, plates, flatware, and glasses, you're quickly consuming that table's real estate.

If you want truly exceptional decor, skip the DIY Pinterest dreams and hire a pro. Like the jaw-dropping creations from all-stars Frank Clemente (a fellow April Fool) and partner Lynn McGee. (When the Super Bowl is in town, they call Frank and Lynn.) Or the extraordinary design crews of 2 Birds, Ideal Designs, Carter's Florist, or SMPL.events. They always seem to be at NOVA, prepping for another wedding. I remind clients all the time to "hire a pro!"

As a young boy, I admit, I played with matches all the time. I recall lighting fires in the vacant lot down the street from our house. I also poured gas on our driveway and lit that up, too. I used to flick matches at everything. I once burned a hole in my sister nurse Julie's dress. She was not happy, at all. It's obvious now why any party of mine that goes past sunset is going to have lots and lots of candles. I love watching fire and flames, and I believe we all do. It's in our DNA.

At NOVA 535, we use oil candles because they are less expensive, greener, and much easier to clean up. Of course, another natural scene enhancer is fresh flowers, which are always a value-added part of your venue's decor; I'll go over that later.

Table Decor

Dinner accouterments that adorn your tables always attract the attention of guests. Plates, glasses, and flatware (silverware) comprise the dinnerware, which can range from simple to elegant. Authentic china plates are heavy, especially if you are carrying stacks of ten from your car to the venue, then back again at the end of the night when you are buzzed and your feet are killing you. Today, we have so many eco-friendly options that it's rare to use real china. Bamboo is a current favorite, or the compostable single-use options. Yet still, you will be consuming and then throwing things away. Speaking as a former Boy Scout and current eco-conscious, tree-hugging human, I cringe when I think of the total volume of trash my industry creates daily. Ugh.

Here's something to consider when you are doing any type of self-service event. If guests are going to be carrying their own plates from a buffet or food truck, position the plates near the food. Position the flatware (forks, knives, spoons, napkins, etc.) at the guests' dining tables. Think for a moment about the weight of the plates, their size, plus all your delicious food piled on top, and then the long walk back to their table. (Excuse me, where was my table again?) Plus, the bumping of elbows and jostling around with other (buzzed) guests along the way. News flash: Guests typically only have two good hands at best. Think in terms of the customer here and carefully plan their dining experience to be enjoyable for them. Lugging heavy dinnerware toward a table, piled high with food, off in a galaxy far, far away, isn't the way to make a good impression with your guests. Also, if the ladies are afraid to abandon their purses at the table, then they are lugging them back and forth along with their plates.

You're going to need napkins, condiments like salt and pepper, and baskets of bread, plus butter, oil, and vinegar. What about water glasses, wine glasses, and champagne flutes? See how quickly the table's real estate got covered. Don't forget second helpings. Unless you prearrange for the waiter or your guests (haha, sure!) to clear their dirty dishes, you can expect to run out of room on the table lickety-split.

Cake and dessert plates, typically around six inches, are just as important as your main course. More napkins, please. Steak, butter, and bread knives? Holy shit. It can spiral out of control quickly, so are you really thinking about teaspoons and tablespoons, too? Since napkins and dishes get dirty, there is always a need for extras. Typically, we add 10 percent to the napkin order and always extra dinnerware and flatware just in case. Seems like there's always a "just in case." Anything goes during live events.

A truly memorable event is about the quality of food, drinks, atmosphere, and entertainment, and the guests' comfort. It's not so much dependent on how many different pieces of silverware you've rented. Personally, I'll take one fork and sharp knife any day, along with a nice, comfy chair, versus fifteen pieces of polished silver and a chair provided by the local chiropractor. Plus, someone has to bus, sort, wash, dry, polish, and organize it all before you go home. Oy vey!

Party Favors and Guest Gifts

In the favors and gifts section, most get silly and wasteful, and only rarely are they thoughtful and practical. My advice is to skip this idea altogether. Spend your money on the best DJ available, like my pal Doug "DJ Fresh" Hensel, who is the DJ for the Tampa Bay Rays Major League Baseball team, or "DJ Jaey" Pereira, who is NOVA's go-to wedding DJ. We love you, Jaey. There's also Mr. not two-times but three-times "Best of The Bay," Neal "DJ Mega" Stoll. And, of course, Tom Shook, aka DJ Dood, along with Mike Rich "DJ Ich," T-Quest, DJ Muggles, DJ Mad Linx, DJ Zeph. . . . Wow, guess I know quite a few. These are my go-to DJs. These guys know how to create a frenzy on the dance floor.

Spend your money on the highest-quality food, good booze, and professional, top-rated vendors and DJs. Skip the silly little things that are most often forgotten—and worse, thrown away in the most eco-unfriendly of ways.

If you feel obligated to do something nice for your favorite people, think in terms of a bottle of vino or, way better in my book, a small, private dinner party to thank your group of core pals personally. Spend those extra few hundred on a hilarious entertainer, singer, skating clown, you get it. Or get a better band, like Helios Jazz Orchestra, hosted by the fantastic David R. Manson or the Bay Kings Band of Tampa Bay; Tori or Brandon will take excellent care of you.

Whatever you choose will have a major impact in terms of gratitude. I think you get what I'm saying: Something very memorable with a few hundred bucks will have the impact you want, compared to those typically meaningless and worthless (to the guests) gifts. Plus, if you are eco-minded at all, think to yourself about how these gifts have a high probability of being just tossed away. Think about that before you order those $3 things made in China for 100 guests. 100 x $3 = $300. Instead, add $150 to your DJ and $150 to your photographer. Skip the eco-unfriendly, dust-collecting junk.

As a guy who hosts a lot of events, I spend most nights cleaning off tables, chairs, bar tops, and my beautiful hardwood floors, collecting and then having to toss countless unwanted "gifts." Some nights, I feel like crying. Like that beautiful Indian in the 1970s anti-littering TV commercial. Save a rainforest, please. They are the lungs of our planet. Instead of spending $300 on shitty little throwaway crap, how nice would it be to donate those dollars to a green charity? Here's an idea. At your sign-in gift table, invite guests to click on the link in their smartphone and donate to their favorite eco-friendly charity. You know, the ones that really does good things for the kids or saves a rainforest. As for gifts to the newlyweds, everyone loves $$Cards$$. From the family's POV, it's the babies everyone is hoping the newlyweds will be making during their honeymoon.

Flowers

Who doesn't love fresh flowers? They are nature's most beautiful artwork. Their look and fragrance contribute a unique ambiance for special events. Flowers aren't right for every occasion—that is, unless you ask my pals Terry and Rod of Carter's Florist here in sunny St. Pete. Holy smokes, can those two create truly magnificent arrangements! They present eye-stopping productions. And Terry sings, too. What a show-off!

Flowers add a simple, gorgeous, elegant, and timeless beautification to every event. It's all about your tastes and budget. A few fresh-cut flowers in a clear glass or bowl, some water, and boom. Your room's vibe goes up a notch. That $150 saved from skipping the eco-unfriendly plastic gifts can be used on some fresh flowers.

After the event ends, the flowers are perfect to take home to a loved one or out for the EOS (end of shift) nightcap as a lure for someone new to canoodle with. I want to send a shout out to my long-time, go-to pro bar team, like superstar bartenders William "Bill" Hoagland, Vanessa Baker, Tara Mutschler, Charlotte Johnson, Kim Rivera, April Johnson, Tasha Clark, Kristy Hay, Lisa Bailey, Lauren Westmoreland, Chris Hamilton, Monique Gerow, Branden Sandahl, Andreas Neuert, Allyson Olaniel, Jason Farrell (Go Rays!), Jenna Shiver, Linda Reschner, Laurene O'Connor, Natalie Gennaro, Justin Rawlings, (Nurse) Rachael Gordon, and, of course, "Big Pete" Peter Quigley. They love taking home fresh flowers! So do our bar-backs Troy Peterson, Troy Peterson and Craig Dobbs. These take-home gifts, full of Mother Earth's wonders, surely have created many a welcome home smile, hug, and hopefully, even some more.

Photographer

We all know every bozo with a smartphone is a photographer, right? *No!* Most everyone snapping pics with their smartphones is clueless. Rule of thirds, right? I test this all the time by asking people to take my phone, and even after I show them the frame and angle I'm looking for. Eighty percent of the time I get garbage.

Seriously, there is a big difference between Joe Schmoe with a smartphone and someone like me, a guy with a Canon 6D who has shot, jeez, over 500,000 images. I take hundreds of photos almost every day. Plus, I do my editing with Lightroom. I have created some really great photos. Patting myself on the back, here. But there is another big drop-off between my skills and the real-deal, high-quality abilities of a true professional master photographer. The people who are trained to capture and edit exceptionally great photos and treasured memories. Like my pal, Brandi Morris, and Sheri Kendrick, for example. Amazing! So are my super helpful travel advice pals. Steven "Thee Photo Ninja" Le and Val Ritter also come to mind; both are also infected with GlobeTrottingTravelitis.

There are a few things critically important for capturing great pictures. The subjects: Are they still or moving? Lighting: Is it partial, harsh, or is there hardly any at all? Is the sun gonna wash things out? Are you capturing a kiss in the candlelight? Or just capturing the candlelight? What about moving objects in the scene, like people dancing? Add in some moving strobe lights. Will you capture their faces or just a messy blur? It's brutally hard to capture great images in low to dark environments, which is the environment where most parties happen. Are you shooting flash against a reflective background like a glass window or a mirror? Our main staircase is wrought-iron, which helps avoid this flashback.

Capture the moment. Is the photographer vigilant and ready to capture those precious moments? Candidly, I use the line, "Hey y'all, let me grab a quick photo" with some wild hand gesturing to get people's attention. I use that a lot. Because if you have more than one person involved, people sitting at a table or standing around chatting, the odds of getting everyone with both eyes open, and a decent smile, in one shot, is like effectively herding cats on meth. It's extremely difficult, and it's vitally important that you hire a seasoned pro. Don't get cheap here. What's that one spectacular photo kept on your mantelpiece worth, decades later? Go to grandma's house and remind yourself that those special moments are priceless.

Pro tip: You can also double up hiring a photog with an amazing personality, like my pals Carol Gallagher, Ann Coffman, and Barry Lively, who add life to your event besides delivering amazing images.

Videographer

The same is also true for a videographer. What style of editing you want? Are you thinking of a thirty-five-minute wedding video that only the bride and groom and maybe their closest family will begrudgingly watch once? No! Think about movie trailers—say three minutes, max. They are super cool. The ones that make you think, *Wow, I wish I was there!*

Don't forget to get everything in writing, including when you expect to get the raw footage and edited final cut(s). How long? What format? What level of HD, 2K, or 4K? Is there audio? Who is being mic'd up? How is that audio being captured? Is the music royalty-free? If not, you've got (more) problems. Also, who owns the raw footage and the final product? You? Or the photographer/ videographer?

We had a fight with some scumbag videographers who kept footage that was (is) legally ours. Fuck-wads and blackmailers. Make it crystal clear in writing that you own all the footage and you have the rights to use it in any way you want. Don't learn the hard way, like I did. They've lost not only my friendship and access into my NOVAverse; they've also lost all of those opportunities to shoot my events. I'll never pay for (100 percent of) everything in advance. No way. Maybe I'll go to 25 percent to maybe 50 percent in advance, and then they have the financial incentive to complete the work correctly and on time. Pay the balance only after you are 100 percent satisfied.

Linens

Linens are pretty much a necessary evil. When you are at a venue, like NOVA 535, for example, you'll find tables that are easily mobile and stackable. Yet they look ugly when naked. No one wants to look at grandma's legs. Well, I use that example to describe why the linens should always be to the floor, covering the ugly (sorry, Grams) legs that need to be kept hidden. So that means linens. Lots and lots of them.

Luckily for me and our team, we have a 5-Star partner, Linens by the Sea, who are a sub of U.S. Tent, located in beautiful Sarasota, Florida. U.S. Tent is owned by my college pal and once upon a time wild and crazy guy, Tim Boyle. We met through a mutual USF graduate-student friend, a guy named Olivier Lamouroux. (Hammm-burrr-gerrr!)

The story of how Olivier and I met involves a guy with a strong French accent, and two lovely ladies. Three people, all on one wheelchair, spinning precariously around the center of the dance floor. Talk about legendary! The story also involves something called the Black Scholes Pricing Model. Woo, those days were crazy. Brains, livers, and boundaries got stretched, pushed, and tested to the max. I am glad that Tim and I got our acts together, finished our college degrees, and now are providing great value for our clients and communities. As for Olivier, he's roaming the streets somewhere east of Cassis, searching for his missing group leader.

Tables, Chairs, Stages, and Other Rentals

If your venue doesn't have everything you need, you'll need a great rental company. Pay attention here. It's easy to try to "save" one to two dollars per chair. That seems to make sense, right? Oh, but you say you want clean chairs, too? Chairs never get spilled on, puked on, or pissed on during events, do they? Disgusting! Thinking about padded seats? Oh, but your butt is gonna hate your cheap ass. I've mentioned that we use U.S. Tent, plus our pal Jesse Caya at Coast to Coast Rentals, PKS Rentals, and, of course, the venerable Howard at Rent-All City. They're all great guys and super reliable, seasoned pros.

Of course, the first question for you is, where are your rental items being dropped off at? Unless it is discussed (in writing), all your stuff could end up on the sidewalk. Who is responsible for the equipment once it's delivered, and who pays for the set-up? Time equals money. Is your floor-plan set and ready to accommodate those 150 seats you ordered? Are the chairs properly spaced? Is there room between and in front of each chair? Those thick asses need wiggle room down those isles.

Your chairs should be delivered and stacked, hopefully inside and close to where they will ultimately be used. When you have 150, 200, or 250-plus guests, that means a lot of unstacking, carrying, and setting up, all neatly in rows or perfectly spaced around tables. Shoot, how many people are there at this table? Where are those stupid table numbers? Why are the pads all torn and discolored? Those chairs don't look white to me. *Help!*

See how quickly this one little detail can quickly swerve out of control just because you're trying to save $1.50 a chair? Who is counting all the chairs upon arrival? Our all-star team at NOVA 535, James, Shawn, Craig, Chris, and Ruby, make sure that 150 ordered means 150 delivered. Who cares if it's just a few short, right? I mean, it *looks* like 150 chairs until Grandma is beating you with her walker, screaming in her nearly forgotten voodoo dialect about the two missing chairs from her only daughter's wedding. Have you ever read *Thinner* by Stephen King? Like all deliveries and inventory, count everything going in and out.

Suppose they are delivered covered in sticky messes and then left 50 meters away from where you need them. Maybe you can ask the already two-sheeted bridal party for some (pun) ASSistance. Correct? No. It's important to research and hire proven pros only. Like team NOVA 535.

We consider our vendors our teammates. They're like family. Jeez, it's just like a marriage. The first rule is to pick an all-star team for your events. (We'll talk more about this and the dreaded rental pick-ups in my "Aftermath" chapter. Here is the bottom-line takeaway: hire a proven pro.)

Entertainment

Yeah, your entertainment is critical. Don't get cheap. Spend more on a proven pro, not an untested flake. I made that mistake early on, and my attempt at saving a few hundred dollars backfired, as the wackadoo entertainer decided, after arriving late, "this gig just isn't for me," and blazed. Ugh! You always want the real pro who shows up ready to perform and deliver 4.5 or 5-Star service, even if her arm was sawed off two days before. (Kidding, but you feel me, yes?)

If you are lucky enough to know one, use someone who can multitask, and hire them for the night. Like my favorite pal, the exquisite Mayven Missbehavin. Beautiful, smart, warm, and friendly. She's a singer, burlesque and go-go dancer, aerialist, fire performer, and much more. She's so hot—she is literally on fire four nights a week. Even when she isn't performing, people just want to be near her because she's a star.

Pole dancers are talented gymnasts using a single twenty-foot vertical pole, and they are amazing. They can also be strippers, but not necessarily. Let's be honest, when you hear "pole dancer" what comes to mind? Plus, who doesn't enjoy a beautiful lady slowly, elegantly, removing her clothing? (Or gent, although I've yet to see a male pole dancer—willingly!) If you say you don't, you should ask yourself, "Why not?"

Here are some of my all-time favorite types of entertainment, along with a few talented entertainers whom I personally recommend.

Go-Go Dancers. Of course, the role of a go-go dancer is just that. It's her role. The human filling that role either makes it spectacular or a train wreck. I like to include a few go-go dancers at any event that expects people to dance. When there are beautiful ladies spinning around on the dance floor, they usually aren't out there alone for very long. Also, burlesque is fantastic. Many of these incredibly talented ladies will do both, if you're lucky. (Riquette Ramsey, Mayven Missbehavin, Gemma Lux, Emily Beck, Christine "Stevie Mistine" Machado, Kayla Maynap, Kissa Von Addams, Ayne Cole, Carmen Lai Garden, Holly Hasty, and the incredible Katie James.)

Skating Evil Clowns. Sam Davis and Dustin Allen-Davis are incredibly talented—and frightening. I love saying, "Skating Clowns!"

Aerialists. (Including Mayven Missbehavin, Riquette Ramsey, Jessica Watson , Taylor Roberts, and Kaley Gay of Aerial Dragons, and Andrea Tirrella.) We sometimes hire these gorgeous ladies to pour champagne for our guests while hanging from the ceiling. Our aerialists are super crowd pleasers at NOVA 535. Our open, sixteen-feet-from-the-ground ceilings are perfect for hanging beautiful ladies from; we do it as often as possible. Yes, that's how we roll.

Speaking of rolling, NOVA's Strolling Tables are round tables, five to six feet in diameter, with a hole cut in the center. This is where a human performer is located. Then they "stroll" around your event with food or drinks on their table. Of course, they are costumed to match your affair. Ours were designed and costumed by the amazing Teresa Parks of Fairwarning, built by superman Mietek Badzinski.

Dueling Pianos. (Rockin' Pianos are incredible. A special thank you to Jeanne and Kevin Milkey!)

Musicians. (Tori Fuson, Brandon C. Williams, Ken Apperson, Dr. David Mansion, Pete Harrison, Betty Lou Fox, Lisa Casalino, Michael Lynch, Sasha Tuck, Margo Ray, Gloria West, and accordionist extraordinaire Nick Boutwell.)

Tarot Card Readers. (Ani Crane).

Face Painters and Makeup Artists. (Corine Potter, Cylin McDonnie and Alin Leslie).

Stilt Walkers. (Holly Havok).

Massage Service. For everyone who is sore the next day, we have sorely needed massage service ladies, Lisa O'Connor and Zoe Schriver.

Stage Magicians and Illusionists. (A dazzling star, the lovely and talented Ms. Erika Cain, who also performs as Gypsy Allure.)

Live Paintings. (Don Kobasky.)

Walk-Around Magic. (Hollywood-bound Mr. Cory Van Valin.)

Balloon Guy. (Mark Byrne, absolutely incredible.)

Katy Perry Impersonator. (The beautiful, smart and talented Stacey Barlow.)

There are so many types of entertainment to include, but you get the drift here, just hire a pro to host your event like we did with world-famous entertainer Sheldon Blake for NOVAween 12. He was fabulous! We love using some fantastic entertainment companies like Breezin Entertainment, Aerial Dragons, Dance and Circus Arts, Casino Party Planners, Moving Arts of Tampa Bay, and Dan Mar Productions. That leaves the best for last, my hilarious family of entertainers over at Got Jokes? Improv.

Props for my brother from another mother, Daniel "Motown" Jefferson, and his creation, Got Jokes?

Entertainment. Wow, where do I begin? I've always loved TV game shows, being a child of the 1970s and exposed to *Hollywood Squares*, *The Dating Game*, *The Gong Show*, *The Price is Right*, *Let's Make a Deal*, and so on. I've always dreamed of creating or hosting one. After Daniel and I met, we soon decided to create, promote, produce, and host a live game show at NOVA 535. *The Big Bang Show* was a combination of *America's Got Talent* and *Whose Line Is It Anyway?* We ran for four seasons—about two calendar years. It was magical.

The Big Bang Show cast was incredible. Fucking hilarious. The Got Jokes? improv comedians and crew included Chuck Glass, Ricky Wayne, Michael "Gwiggy" McGuigan, Tarik Lewis, Barry "HBO" Naylor, Sharon Nolan, David "DeTyme" Tolliver, Allen "Rocky" Cusseaux, Davell Taylor, Heidi Lux, Ali "That Girl," plus music grooves from DJ Ace Vedo and DJ Ich (Mike Rich).

I was one of the three judges. Besides myself, the judges were Mike E. Graf and a rotation of local celebrities, including fitness Entrepreneur Forbes Riley, tough guy CJ Johnson, "Mr. Theatrical" Sterling Powell, and radio star Ali "That Girl." Our job was to give honest, raw feedback to the five contestants. Five performers, such as singers, acrobats, magicians, bands, unique performers, spoken word artists, whatever, competed for a $1,000 cash prize, and the winner was chosen by audience applause. We three judges would select the Wild Card (second place) at each show. Then the Wild Cards battled for a spot in the Grand Finale. Our final show of the season pitted the best against the best, leaving only one performer standing to be crowned the Big Bang Show Champion and the recipient of a check from NOVA for $1,000. Comedian Chuck Glass was Season One's winner. That's how he got invited to join Got

Jokes. Chuck returned a few years later to NOVA 535 and married his beautiful sweetheart, Sofia. (What a cool, superhero-themed wedding they had!)

So, here I was, live-judging, making things up on the spot with my buddy, Daniel, and co-producing the show while also running the event, the video equipment, and the venue itself. Unfortunately, this was right before the explosion of excellent video on smartphones. We have some episodes up on YouTube, sadly not doing the show justice. Search Michael S. Novilla and *The Big Bang Show* at NOVA 535. #SolidGold.

On our first *Big Bang Show* episode, we were really green and just figuring things out on the fly. The inspiration for the idea came from *The Gong Show* and the occasion when my pal, Chris Skeie, mentioned my dream to create and host a live game show. He loved the hard-ass gong that the judges or host rang when an act sucked ass. The premise was that not everyone is good, and not everyone deserves a round of applause. It just so happens that some people are terrible. Well, we gonged the first really bad act, and that guy got all pissed off and walked out right in the middle of the show. We felt terrible and decided that we wanted to be honest and direct yet still encouraging.

Interestingly I saw a Facebook post recently with a *Big Bang Show* first-season female comedian contestant, Catherine Maloney. She did great and got some real heartfelt encouragement and honest pointers about how to improve. In fact, she implemented them into her act. This recent post featured Catherine thanking everyone, including me, fellow comedian Christine O'Leary, and Daniel Jefferson, for believing in and encouraging her. The pointers she received that night inspired her to improve, work hard, and never give up. A decade later, we can all celebrate with laughter at the incredible journey of comedienne Catherine Maloney. #HonestFeedback.

Chapter 11

Floorplans and Flow Plans

How many guests are you inviting?

What would Goldilocks say is the magic number of guests that makes your event just right? That depends on a lot of factors. Are you hosting a public event where you're making money from bar and ticket sales? If so, then you want to max out the number of guests. On the other hand, is it your mom's seventieth birthday? For that event, the Goldilocks number is the total number of the closest family and friends who will share their love and support for yo momma. For corporate events, the Goldilocks recommendation is typically the staff or staff plus one.

You can create a guest list and instruct the doorman to check all arriving guests by name, plus photo ID, as they enter. Does your venue provide a doorman? Is he a day laborer with a freshly dug-up look, or is he professionally trained, licensed, and insured? Let's review the three types of events:

Invite Only: Not on the list means no entrada.

Invited +1: Your invited guests can bring their own guest(s).

Open to the Public: Of course, any open to the public event is, well, open to the public. The host can impose legal restrictions on age. That can be categorized as kids only, teens only, seniors only, eighteen years old and up, or legal drinking age and up, (which, typically, here in the USA, is twenty-one years of age).

Do you want to provide a seat for every "arse"? That's an important question. Have you considered assigning seats to some or all your guests? (Please don't. It's a nightmare.) Are you considering assigning tables with guests seated at their assigned tables?

I have found that it's usually unnecessary to assign guests to specific seats at their tables. The only real exception is when you are serving custom-plated meals to tables. Still, even then, you have the choice to give guests individual seating cards that they will put on the table they're assigned to and for the seat they prefer. For smaller events, maybe up to thirty guests, you can assign seats, but it's gonna be a lot of trouble. Assigning guests to specific tables works great with a pro caterer, as they can serve the guests' pre-selected meals—typically only two to three choices max (beef, fish, or veggie, for example)—right at the tables. The server arrives at the table, looks at the place card or, worst case, just asks, "Who has the vegetarian?" and delivers the meal right to the guest.

If your mind's made up on assigning guests to specific tables, then I suggest a cool way to make it fun. We've had clients name their tables after films, like at Hollywood and TV-themed events. Some clients choose tables identified with planets associated with *Star Wars*, *Dune*, or other sci-fi themes. Some clients name tables after famous streets or for countries that have some association with their guests. The all-French table, bonne nuit!

If you want designated people to sit with certain other people, then it's best to assign groups of between two and twelve together at Table #1. Assigning guests to specific seats is a true nightmare, and we work hard to recommend alternatives to any client who requests that option. The math is insane, especially after people have RSVP'd and then notify the host they are not coming after all, but a day before the event date, give another notice that, well maybe they will come after all. Some people want to be seated next to each other as a couple. The problem is, something can happen in their relationship, and you will then be stuck with either an empty seat or two red-faced humans who definitely do not want to be seated next to each other that evening.

The takeaway is to keep it simple. Assign your guests to tables rather than seats, if you feel you must at all. The randomness of no table assignments introduces just the right amount of anticipation and excitement to your event. Many people meet their spouses—as well as their future ex's—at a friend's wedding or special event. As a host or event planner, you have plenty of other things to focus on. Bottom line: Do not assign guests to seats, only to tables, if you must.

Chapter 12

The Month (30 Days) Before Your Event

Final Vendor Confirmations

Okay, let's assume you booked your event months ago and you're following all my excellent advice. As you approach the one-month date before your event, you are in good shape.

Your event summary timeline is:

Venue

2020-12-28 1:00 pm - 4:00 PM Set-Up
(Vendors Only)
2020-12-28 4:00 pm - 10:00 PM Your Event Name
(Guests allowed)
2020-12-28 10:00 pm - 11:30 PM Break Down and
Clean Up (EON)

Set-Up and Break-Down

It's all about the details. Who is providing which goods and services? For example, the mother of the bride (MOB) is bringing homemade centerpieces and a supply of candy for a candy bar. What time should they arrive? Who will be setting these items up? How exactly should the setup look? Hint: Have them set up at home and send you high-quality photos. Many smartphones allow screen writing, so you can easily label and show exactly how they want it. Where will this item's boxes be stored during your event?

You've assigned the Venue Manager (aka "day of" coordinator) to set the candy bar items up. Who will be refilling that candy during the event and keeping the table clean from trash? Who is breaking those items down after the event? Answer: The catering company has agreed to manage it during the event, then break all the candy bar items down and put them back into the boxes provided by MOB after the event concludes. Who is expected to take those items home with them? Answer: MOB's best GF (whose name and cell number is . . . ?) is taking the leftover items home with her. See what I mean here? It's more work up front, but much less stress and headache later—when everyone is buzzed and tired—when you have all these details planned out and part of your written timeline. Apply this same planning model to catering, beverages, lighting, sound, decorations, gifts, etc. Who is responsible for delivering, setting up, breaking down, storing the items in boxes, then taking things home?

Please make sure to save the boxes that everything (that is going home) came packed in. Just ask our excellent venue managers Melissa Nguyen, Ruby Thomas Dolce, James Greenwalt, and my brother Chris Novilla about the difference between an organized event versus an night-mare unplanned event. Storing the boxes right under the six-foot folding tables with linens to the floor is typically best and easiest. The hardest job with the candy bar is that you're walking past it, all night long. Those tasty little sweets call your name as you pass by. It's a sweet whis-per, but I swear I can hear it. Just make sure to wipe your mouth before you go back to talk to your client! I was eat-ing one of those chocolate mustaches, clowning around, and, yup, I wore a huge chocolate mustachio for about an hour. . . . Dork!

Trying to stack multiple glass jars into your messy car trunk, at 3 AM, next to the tire iron and who knows what else is a recipe for broken glass and migraines. If it's going home and not into the recycle, because nothing gets left at the venue—all goes in/out the same day—then save the box. A nice roll of shipping tape is never a bad idea. Plenty of reusable cloth bags can literally save a new mar-riage. Plus, keep in mind the eco-friendliness of it all. More trash = more pollution = sicker humans and wildlife = sad Mother Earth.

Written and Executed (Signed) Expectations

All your vendors should have been hired by now, each with an executed (written and signed) contract, including explicit, easy-to-understand, written expectations detail-ing exactly:

What they are expected to do in detail, so there is zero confusion by anyone.

When (what time) each part of those expectations is to happen. When do they arrive? When do they perform? When are they on break? When do they depart? When are first and last payments due? When is the cake being delivered?

Exactly **where** (location) each element of the agreement happens. Be specific. For example, cake is to be placed on top of the thirty-six-inch round table located in the north-west corner of the ground-floor main gallery. The cake is to be cut by the catering company, who is also providing cake cutter, white cocktail napkins, and six-inch dessert plates. Guests will serve themselves cake after the cake is removed from the thirty-six-inch cake table and brought to bar #3 to be cut and placed on caterer-supplied dessert plates. Plates with cake slices to be arranged on the granite top of bar #3.

How much does each component cost? A detailed invoice with price per unit, item descriptions, and totals, taxes, fees—everything resulting in the 100 percent total amount due. No hidden fees or service charges.

How long will each part of the event be (when applicable)? For example, musicians play three sets of thirty minutes with two fifteen-minute breaks. What happens during those breaks? Who is responsible for the break-time music? Who decides what is being played, who provides those songs, who pushes start and stop, what type of music files, what device, what is it being plugged into, and what is it being powered by? Does that device need a stand? What kind of stand? Cause everyone will be taking photos of that band. Seriously, think like you are talking to kinder-garteners. Not that your vendors are stupid or anything, but just keep things step-by-step clear so that anyone can understand.

Explain all defined responsibilities. Such as who is to deliver everything on the day of, do the set-up, manage during the event, break down after the event, and then remove them at the end of the event. You will have already met with them at your venue and walked through details, including floor plans and timeline. At the final walk-through, actual or virtual, you are giving vendors your final head count and any other final instructions, which, for NOVA 535, is due thirty days before the event. Generally, this is the time to finalize everything.

From a date thirty days before until fourteen days before the event, that's the time to review and double-check everything. At the fourteen-day point before your event, lock everything down for real. Then review your final head count, detailed floor plans, and inventory of linens and supplies so you can make any last-minute special orders, etc.

Call Your Key People and Influencers

If your event is open to the public and you are counting on ticket sales and expect some guests to bring their own guests, then you need to call all of your KPI's (key persons of influence). You need to identify those people—assuming you've invited them, of course—who know and influence others. Like my long-time mentors and friends, Jon "Reno" LaBudde, Doug "DJ Fresh" Hensel, Rosey "Indie Market" Williams, Marina "ArtPool" Williams (related only in their awesomeness!), John Vitale, Sheldon Blake, Olga Bof, and Jeff "Grown Folks" Copeland. Like the oracle, you want to have their blessing and help when you're throwing a party that's open to the public.

At the thirty-days-out point, at least here in sunny St. Pete, ticket sales are typically slow even for events that run every year, like my NOVAween Halloween Costume Party. People like to wait until just a few weeks before to RSVP. Shoot, most will wait until a few days before to buy their tickets, even if we offer saving incentives. It's the nature of the beast. So, at thirty days, don't panic over your low advanced ticket sales. Just keep pushing them, and make sure your influencers continue promoting the event. Have your event flyer as the cover image for you and your influencers' FB and IG pages and profiles. Place a "Buy Tickets" link in social media threads and email signatures, etc. Keep reminding everyone that this is a must-attend event.

Facebook event attendees are only a gauge. It's super easy to click a "Like" or "Going to" on a page or event, but purchasing a ticket with real, hard-earned money is something else. It's possible to have 400 "attending" people on FB with 10 actual ticket sales. What people say they are doing and what they actually do can be wildly different.

Send out event announcements with incentives for guests to save $10 (or whatever makes sense) by purchasing tickets online in advance. That might be $30 good until August 31, one month before the October 1 event. September 1, the price bumps up to $40 online until online sales end, say, two to twenty-four hours before your event. Then tickets are available at the door for $50.

Don't forget about the collection of applicable sales tax. I've been audited by the Florida Department of Revenue, and it's a nightmare. Even when you are doing everything (you think) perfectly and within the law, the tax laws are almost impossible to follow correctly, so you had better get professional advice and pay every nickel you owe in sales tax. Get yourself a superstar CPA, like I did with Mickey Japp and King Kong CPA Charlie Santana, who just retired. Do a sales tax review audit if you are even slightly involved in anything to do with paying sales tax.

Expect to find people in a rush to buy their tickets at the last minute. Have your easy online ticketing system working well up until a few hours before the event. You may need those few hours (ahead of time) to list paid and unpaid VIP guests (your mom, the local press, your life partner, best friend, etc.), so the door entry process is smooth and easy. There will always be snags, and people can get lost in the shuffle. I am thinking here of people like your business partner or wife (that's a bummer), so be prepared to add a few names to your (free entry) VIP list in real-time.

This is where spending a bit more of your money and training on a professional doorman comes in most handy. You don't want to be anchored at the door during your event, fighting with a messy clusterfuck of a door entry process, so really work hard on your list and have everything ready in advance to flow smoothly through the door. Do a practice run a few days before. Your VIP list should be alphabetized and on a spreadsheet with four columns:

- Last Name
- First Name
- Notes
- Blank Column for "X" (used by your door-person when checked in)

Have a name on your list for every ticket you sell and/or give away. Let's say your advance online sales list shows Jon Smith, plus three. At the door, Jon Smith appears with only one of his plus-three ticket holders. Or perhaps his plus-two guests arrived early on their own and are friends of Jon's friend, but they don't know Jon or even his last name. By having all their names on your guest list, your doorman will ID all of them as they arrive and keep things flowing without interrupting you for confirmation. Remember, it doesn't matter who buys the ticket; what counts is that Lisa Smith has her photo ID, and Lisa Smith's name is on the VIP list. Hence, she goes right into the venue—assuming Lisa is old enough and Lisa doesn't try sneaking in a quart of booze hidden in her massive purse. Aren't you glad you weren't cheap with your doorman? If you aren't patting down your public event guests and checking purses, bags, and backpacks, then your bar sales will be much lower than expected. This isn't breaking news, folks.

This is important. You want your doorman checking IDs and watching for uninvited wackos. You need at least one doorman at entry step #1, plus some check-in assistants at entry step #2. Check-in people can be seated with a laptop at a six or eight-foot-long rectangular table, or two if there are multiple ticket types, and maybe a VIP table or line for checking in guests after they pass by the doorman. Of course, be sure to have an extension cord with a (working) power strip, plenty of lighting, laptop(s), paper, and several working pens. Make sure your lighting is focused on the table and not in the guests' eyes.

Have an organized system as well as cash for change and credit card resources for those last-minute ticket purchasers. (That's like $100 in $1's, $100 in $5's, $100 in $10's, and

$100 in $20's.) Plus, you've confirmed that your handheld credit card machine(s) are working properly, have plenty of paper, and that the people operating them are well-versed in how they work. Various machines work differently and can cause confusion and delays, which makes guest entry a nightmare. Or they will be queued up and pissed before they even enter your event. Maybe they say "fuck this" and blaze. It happens all the time.

Also, don't forget to settle those CC machines at the end of the night. Don't just turn them off. You need to settle that batch. (Read the instructions or watch a YouTube Video). And make sure you are including sales tax (when applicable) in your ticket price. Round everything to even dollars; no one wants to be fumbling with coins or wads of $1 bills. It's $30 including sales tax. Smooth and easy.

14 Days Before Your Event

Confirm all meals. Confirm how they're being served and where, with notes about any special electric power needs. We use a simple visual method to show your caterer the number of meals needed and how to compute the final head count. We use:

"Event name and date, and dinner serving time"

Headcount for Beverages

Total Guests = Minors (under 21) + Adults

For example:

Minors (under 21) = 30

Adults = 70

Total Guests = 100

Headcount for Food

Kids = 20
Vegetarian = 20
Beef = 35
Chicken = 25
Vendor = 12

Total Meals = 112

Vendor meals can be preselected with a choice for beef or veggie, for example. We get a fix on the total meals required for all humans who will be in the building. Vendors typically get what guests don't take. That means if there are extra beef or chicken servings, the vendors get those. This helps your caterers manage their inventory.

Order Supplies

Under the heading of supplies, I'm thinking spirits, beer, wine, soft drinks, mixers, paper goods, trash bags, etc. In other words, everything on your checklist which has already been carefully prepared along the way, since you are a good student and note-taker. But I recommend waiting to order these items until fourteen days out, because there are always last-minute adjustments—assuming there aren't any special custom-made orders.

Custom orders should be done immediately after final confirmation (in writing) and payment in full. We require all headcounts and payments to be made at thirty days before our NOVA 535 events. Twenty years as a landlord taught me to collect money up front and get everything in writing. Trying to collect money after the event is like chasing a bad dream. You rarely get it all, and it's always frustrating.

Chapter 13

One Week Before Your Event

One week prior to your event, get a massage and plenty of sleep. Avoid those all-nighters, avoid any form of wild partying, and, of course, send to voicemail any friends whose ringtones play, "Shots! Shots! Shots!"

Seriously, take care to eat well, hydrate, exercise, and, most importantly, have a comfy outfit picked out and ready to go for your big event. Wear shoes that are broken in and comfortable. Be sure you are well rested, especially the day before, and abstain from heavy party experiences. In other words, prepare in advance to ensure your physical comfort for the event. If your event is a wedding, think like a good Boy Scout: Be prepared.

Here's a nugget from my own experience. If your event is a wedding and the client (or you) is getting married for the first time, understand that this is going to be a marathon, not a sprint. You must be prepared for all the dinners, cocktails, parties, and after parties, etc, during the week before the actual big day. On event week, food consumption is filled with rich foods, lots of breads, sugars, and heavy stuff that's not good for you. There will be way too much alcohol flowing, and you'll never get those seven hours (minimum) of sleep you need for optimum health.

Be sure to pace yourself. It's a week, not just a weekend. You've gotta be physically, mentally, and emotionally able to hang, dance, and shake your whatever way past midnight on the big day, after a long week, and, if you're out with me, until 5 AM!

Bottom line, as the event planner, host, or guest, it's important to be in the kind of physical shape that permits you to enjoy dancing, laughing and having fun versus having to sit down exhausted, watching everybody else, or worse, being hammered and making an "arse" of yourself. Everyone can hit "record" on their phone, and capture "live" on FB or YouTube, so tomorrow, your career can be over. Getting enough sleep, eating well (fruits and veggies and plenty of clean water), stretching, and at least one brisk walk, are cornerstones for an enjoyable day. That goes for life in general.

Don't forget, you, the guest of honor, or the bride/groom, are the center point of your event. Everyone will be saying "hello," with lots of accompanying handshakes and hugs. It's taxing. Just trying to recall names alone. Remember my rule. It's always, "Nice to see you." I'm bad with recalling names and used to fumble this all the time. I've seen people's unhappy reactions, probably thinking, *What an ass*, when I failed to recall their names. My Achilles heel, in real time, is name recall.

An important part of the week before your event is the obvious: Think through everything about the event one more time. I always try to do that. Things will go wrong. It's a marathon, not a sprint.

Loss of Electrical Power

There's not much you can do if the power company has a downed power line or another infrastructure issue pops up. Maybe you have generators, but doubtful. You can roll the dice only so long unless your power is as reliable as ours is at NOVA. Knock on wood!

It's funny. As I'm typing this in Pokhara, Nepal the hotel power (and Wi-Fi) is ON . . . OFF . . . ON . . . OFF . . . ON several times every day. Ugh! So, when it happens, you do what you can. Do you have plenty of oil candles and lighters? Will losing power affect your bar (not the pouring but the paying) and bathroom services for the guests? For instance, if the power goes down, does your soda gun still work? What about those automatic toilets? Will they still flush? Do you have an old-school battery-powered radio? Or battery power for people to play music off of their phones? You can have backup stores of soda and mixers for your guests.

Think *backups*. Watch a few zombie thrillers, where the power is down for days, and reassess what you can have on-site just in case. Candles, booze, and friends can still create the most memorable of events.

Bad Weather

What is Mother Nature looking like the week before your event? Do you have a rain plan? Are you checking in guests? Is the journey from exiting your vehicle into the venue covered? How long does it take a guest to get checked in? Is there a way to improve that process? Do your valet and doorman have plenty of umbrellas handy? Have you provided a coat rack and coat check option?

Is there an easy ticket system for all those coats? Even a simple roll of those classic, matching tear-off tickets—one for host one for guest—can save the day when you have a hundred coats and jackets. That, and one or two of those easy-to-assemble rolling clothing racks. Trust me.

What about entry mats for those multitudes of wet feet as they enter from rainy, muddy streets? Where are the umbrellas going to be safely stored? A lot of water runs off a wet umbrella. Should you have a contingency plan to rent a tent? You need at least a week, more realistically a few weeks, to get a good tent. During the rainy season, you had better book it a month or more in advance. Ask my brother Tim at U.S. Tent. If it's a hard rain, where is that water flowing to? I hope it's not going into the venue area. Wet dress shoes = frowns. Do a quick check on the grade of your ground outside and around the venue building. Are the storm drains clear or blocked? Do the valet and doorman have their rain plans in order? Discussing this in advance is the smart move. #BadWeatherHappens.

Guests

There will always be last-minute additions or subtractions on the guest list. The reasons are often due to their kids' issues, illnesses, deaths in their families, hitting the bong a bit too hard at home, etc. Occasionally, these no-shows turn out to be key people. If so, then their roles must be reassigned. Like, right now.

Suppose an important speech has been scheduled to be given by a no-show guest. What then? You may also have to make new seating adjustments, timeline alterations, etc., in response to RSVP updates that came in at the last moment.

And they do. Do you have extra chairs, dinnerware, and napkins for your "surprise guest" in from Montana?

Vendors

Worse, the no-show may be your valet company. When it's pouring rain, that could leave a hundred pissed off corporate guests waiting in front of your venue. Ask my brother from another mother, a most incredible human being, adventure chef extraordinaire Brent Shaver, about the night we met at NOVA 535. And how we became the best of friends when he immediately jumped outside in the pissing rain to help me park cars because the fucking valet company was a no show. That night, NOVA lost the biggest account we'd had to date, just six months into business.

One simple mistake like a no-show vendor can ruin your event. And possibly your business. We lost well over $100K in revenues from that single no-show vendor. Think I'm paranoid about double-checking everything? Yes! Get on the phone two weeks before and make sure your vendors and guests are ready, willing, and able to perform their duties on the day of.

Check with your vendors at least twice to make sure they are on the same page with you regarding the menu for the event, head counts, timelines, and their drop-off and pick up schedules. Go over with them exactly what they are and are not required to bring to the event and confirm that they must pick up everything just after the event ends. Go over exactly where they are and aren't parking.

Here's a reminder: You need to have all this clearly planned out and agreed upon with your vendors in writing, so at the end of the event, you are not dealing with a no-show third-party delivery company. Trust me—you will not be in the shape or mood to be making decisions about pickup and answering, "Can we get our stuff next week?" Hey, the answer is always, "No." Put it all in writing, with clearly defined expectations. Every single time, without exception. Last time I made an exception, my video was kept by those asshole videographers. Still haven't seen it. Ugh! Everything in writing and signed by everyone.

Have a clear understanding with vendors that everything is scheduled for pickup when the event ends. Then it's done and over. You won't have to deal with vendors in the next day's vampire-killing sunlight. Nope. No way. The day after is for recoup time, a leisurely brunch, lunch, or dinner, and maybe a massage and pressed juice rehydration therapy. Your day-after energy and mood will not be ripe for arguing or waiting for vendors to come back and get their wares.

> **IT'S 5AM GO HOME**
>
> When you're working with NOVA 535, all the answers are right there on your phone. Our MyNovaEvent.com system provides access for all our clients and vendors. It has arrival schedules, a list of vendors, everyone's contact info and their role(s), the event timeline, floor plans, venue map, and details about the bar, linens, lighting, sound; it has everything.

Make sure your entertainment knows what time they are scheduled to arrive and what time they are performing. You don't want to be dealing with setup tasks, clueless entertainers, and last-minute questions, and especially not sound checks, while your event is running. All entertainers must understand exactly when they are scheduled to arrive, where they should park, where in the venue they can get ready, where they are performing, for how long, and what happens during their breaks. Also, they must know how they are breaking down because their set may end before your event does, sometimes hours before. What happens then? No one wants a ladder hauled into the middle of your dinner party to remove the aerialist rigging, do they? This potential calamity can be avoided if you have all these questions answered and agreed upon in advance.

One of our DJs was given a specific list of songs to play and which songs not to play. In advance, everyone was on the same page. Bravo! That's different from "play classic rock, blues, and R&B, just no rap or country," which is still fine, as long as it's done in advance. Then the DJ is ready to party. Many clients are waiting until the week before or, even worse, the day of to finalize song lists. This is a huge no-no. It produces stress for everyone and greatly increases the chance for errors and mistakes. The NOVA Way is to push for all decisions to be made and finalized at thirty days out. Yes, that's far out, but when you have a rule for a hard deadline and the seven-days-away time arrives, all you have left to do are itsy-bitsy final tweaks. That's so nice. Remember: the DJs don't have every song and every version on their laptops, and bands and musicians have to actually learn and practice new songs.

Sound checks, in advance, are a must. NOVA requires all our bands and entertainers use NOVA's in-house sound system. Our NOVA AV system—thank you Chuck Taylor at Production Source—is set up so that the sound is awesome in every room, including our award-winning restroom suites! Bands are notorious for bringing a few ugly speakers on stands and setting their monitors on the floor/stage. Often with some horrible throw rug tossed over all those cords.

It's like the sawdust that gets tossed over puke at a carnival; lipstick on a pig. That means all the sound comes blaring directly at the crowd, not beautifully mixed throughout the venue like we have. Plus, they look terrible in photos and have trip-hazard cords running everywhere. What a mess.

Unlike the rest of us, band members are generally hard of hearing. "Huh?" Playing rock 'n' roll five nights a week does that to them. They play louder than what makes sense for the room they're in. You should schedule times (with the band leader) during the event when guests can have normal conversations and relax a bit during cocktail hour and during dinner. Sure, there are times when you want the bass thumping and everyone out on the dance floor with the volume set to max, but as part of your preparations, have the band sound-tested in your venue, and make it crystal clear to the leader that they are obligated to follow your or your venue manager's sound level instructions for the entire event. Bands need to pay attention and be alert as you point to your ears and give them an up or down signal with the thumb, directing them to raise or lower their sound levels. Watch your guests to see if they have to yell to be heard. There's a time to talk and a time to dance.

DJs can be difficult to deal with. I've had many who made me repeat my instructions for them over and over and over again. "Turn the fucking volume down! People can't hear themselves think!" It's a cocktail hour, not a rave. Screaming over loud music can be especially troublesome for a holiday party or wedding event; volume must match the event schedule.

I, as the day-of venue manager, walk around our venue during the event, checking temperature and sound, asking and observing, watching and paying attention, to my guests. I check from above and among the crowds. I ask the ladies about the temp and everyone about the volume. I have frank conversations with the band and DJ when we meet, especially during the month, and then again on the day of set-up, regarding sound levels. It is important for these guys to be crystal clear that you (or your manager) are the boss. They need to know their sound levels are under your control, not theirs.

Set aside time and have real conversations with your vendors the week of so they can confirm their arrival times and the event start-and-end times. Also confirm with all of them, who is bringing exactly what and how many—dishes, plates, napkins, mixers, (no straws, as they end up feeding our fish), ice, garbage bags, etc. Keep in mind that all it takes to ruin an event is for the cake lady to show up two hours too early (melted ice-cream cake) or, worse yet, two hours late. What if the caterer makes food from your first draft menu rather than from your final event menu? Umm, it would really be a bummer if the caterer didn't see the last-minute menu update about no onions because the groom is allergic. (Yeah, that happened.)

Or imagine if the caterer somehow missed your note about needing twenty-five more guest meals. Oh, and they also fumbled with including the seventeen vendors as well. Try telling the DJ and photographer there isn't any food for them. That's a fun conversation. Then go tell your doorman and security team the news that there ain't no chow. Hope you are fast on your feet. You can see why it's important to confirm all meals, how they're being served, plus where and exactly when they are to be served. Don't forget to discuss any extra or unusual electric power needs, do a final floorplan review, and check any other final on-site details.

Did someone bring the ice? Don't ASS-U-ME. Be 100 percent sure.

Chapter 14

The Day of Your Event

Okay. Beginning at the "thirty days before" date we've been sharing from the fountain of knowledge, the day of your event is here.

Wowzers! Are we ready? Duh. Of course we are because we are modeling from the NOVA Way.

In the "pregame" hours before your event, if you feel like you need a drink, be smart here. You can drink if you must, but be careful. Indulge only a little bit; stick to wine, beer, or cider. It's better to do that. Even better is nothing at all, until the event itself starts. Make sure you set aside time to have a good, healthy meal prior to your big event. If you've booked a venue like NOVA 535, you can get ready right at our venue. But if you must travel, be sure to factor in your travel time and add a little cushion. Please rideshare or taxi yourself there. When you arrive at your venue, you'll exit from the back seat fresh, smiling, and relaxed.

Seriously, eat a big, healthy lunch on the big day. (This goes for the client, as well—especially if a bride is involved.) No one wants to deal with an upset stomach. It's so easy, even for us professional partiers, to get swept up in, "Sure, pour me a glass of bubbly," early in the day. Then, sooner than expected, you find yourself giving an easy "yes" to that second, overpoured glass of wine from your best friend. Then, a bit later, "hell yeah," comes out of your mouth to the question, "just a little shot?" Oh, and that third drink comes at about 1:00 PM, and, let's see, your ceremony is at 6:00 PM #TrainWreck.

I've been hosting my Entrepreneur Social Club almost every Thursday night since 2009, and I never drink until long after the event has started, usually waiting until the meeting is over and we're at dinner. I never want to think I need a drink to relax or provide me with false confidence. #NoCrutches. There was enough of that in my teens and twenties.

Once your event has started—and the valet is parking cars, and the doorman, DJ, and catering company are all in full swing—then you can grab yourself drinkey numero uno.

There's no pressure on you (sarcasm) just because all your friends, family and photo-takers are at the big event and counting on you. It's your day. Your photos will be published all over social media, all over everywhere.

For your event, be sure to wear comfortable shoes. You'll be on your feet for a long, long, time, and your arches would like to make you feel comfy, in your favorite shoes, all broken in. When it comes time to dance, #ImYourBoogieMan.

Chapter 15

Event Time, Let's Party!

Now that the event is finally here, you feel the butterflies in your belly. It's showtime! Your preparations are complete. Lighting, sound, and decor are set, and the catering team is happily working away. You've checked, and the bartenders are sober and ready to begin pouring. Your doorman and valet are accounted for. The DJ, band, and entertainers have completed their sound checks, warmups, and so on. Yeah, baby. It's party time.

You've done your walk-through to confirm that the lighting is perfect, candles are lit, and the music is playing. Then you think, *OMG! Is there toilet paper in the stalls?* Yes. The staff is accounted for and doing their thing, all properly dressed, smelling fresh and clean—no perfume or cigarette stench. No chewing gum.

You stop to take a big, deep breath and smile. You're ready to welcome guests. Remember the trick I use at the door to greet guests? I say, "Nice to see you," instead of, "Nice to meet you." I've literally heard someone say to me—and, holy shit, did I feel like an ass—"Mike, we've met three times before." Ugh! "Nice to see you."

At many of our NOVA events, I like to play photographer. This gives me permission to interact with everyone, and I love to get great photos, anyway. Then I am in control of those valuable memories—blogs, social media, you understand. So, I walk around, entering and exiting conversations at will. I can choose to linger and have lots of small talk with one set of folks or just say a quick "hi" to others.

I am always on a tight hosting schedule. NOVA is a big place with lots of areas and corners, inside and out, lights, and mini-atmospheres to manage like a party gardener. Most weeks, we have multiple events scheduled that keep me super busy. Plus, I'm always promoting and hosting my Entrepreneur Social Club. At some point, even my motor-mouth gets a little talked out. My role-playing as event photographer gives me permission to multitask and circulate among our guests. I can also play bartender if I feel like it and still get great shots with my camera while meeting all the requirements of a great host.

Of course, for those who host only a few events each year or even one event a year, this role model of photo-gadfly probably isn't your first option. My multiple-personality role-playing mostly works for those of us who are in the ironman live event production world. You will appreciate what I mean when you find yourself scheduling and running up to five events each week. Oh, and did I forget to mention the art of juggling hundreds of clients, thousands of vendors, and tens of thousands of guests, with the predictable drama and chaos that comes with a 5-Star event business model? It's insanity!

Many of you probably just want to be prepared to host one or two events a year, or maybe even that one special wedding or fiftieth anniversary. Your priority is to really make each occasion as perfect as possible. That's okay. Remember to have your smile on and to appear fresh and ready to go as you welcome your guests to their best event experience ever. You are their host who makes it happen.

You have the option to have someone else greet your guests. You can find someone super special for greeting guests, especially at events with large guest lists. Hire a local actor or two. Those few hundred dollars saved from skipping the crappy, eco-unfriendly, no-thank-you gifts could be spent on a pro doorman. People love them. Obviously, a bride or groom should delegate those tasks to someone who is skilled at graciously helping people to their seats, finding the bar, restrooms, etc. A nice warm welcome takes that little edge off the tension at the start of big events. We all have those subliminal tensions from our high expectations when entering a new space, especially one with strangers.

Once guests are inside your home or venue, provide them with the opportunity for a welcome drink. Consider having someone offer glasses of red or white wine, or maybe a flute of bubbly to "wet their whistle," as my grandmother, Ethelynn Gleiss Williams Clark, used to say. Or, at the very least, point your guests in the direction of the bar (and restrooms), and introduce them to your bartender.

Umm, don't forget about smells. It's your job to make sure your home or venue doesn't have any mysterious odors. No stinky! Never allow smoking inside your venue, ever. Just ask smokers to go outside, as there should never, ever be any smoking inside. I refuse to allow ashtrays or dead cigs inside NOVA 535. We don't clean with harsh chemicals, we won't use toxic sprays, and there are no air perfumes used inside NOVA—especially no air fresheners.

At NOVA, we believe the smell of nothing but fresh air is best for our guests. If there is something baking in the oven for the event, like fresh bread, that's fine.

Nightmare Scenarios

Your monkey mind, the bane of all yoga people, along with the possibility of real scenarios, can ruin your mood, dissolving your positive hosting confidence big time. Think of these worries as a sort of stage fright that event planners and hosts go through to earn their bones. Here's a taste:

"OMG, the sky is suddenly getting darker by the minute. Oh, shit. Where are all those clouds coming from? Is that rain? Damn, it's starting to pour outside. We can hear it. Was that lightning? WTF?"

Your phone rings. The VIP guests' bus has a flat tire.

TEXT: Your best friend can't make it, she thinks she has food poisoning.

TEXT: Your special out-of-towners got the event date all wrong.

TEXT: The guest of honor's kids have severe tummy aches.

"The sitter hasn't shown up yet. Can you believe it?"

The city decided to start street repairs right outside your front door today. Look, the sidewalk and right-of-way are a war zone.

A big ass delivery truck for the business next door just pulled up in front of your driveway, and they are slowly unloading what looks like an entire store's worth of goods.

There's a three-car accident. First responders are driving back and forth with sirens blaring. They are out front right now, blocking your guests' access.

Someone just out of sight is yelling "Holy Shit!! The building next door looks like it's on fire!!"

The room feels like it's spinning. You need to sit down. A panic attack is percolating. Your head starts to ache. Is anyone going to show up?

"Wait. . . . Shit, man, the lights are flickering." Now you just lost power. And you were already low on ice.

As the owner and operator of NOVA 535, the hundred-year-old building in downtown St. Pete, at one time or another, I've imagined, or faced, all of these nightmares . . . and some others I just cannot share.

We've had our wireless mic stop working mid-sentence during ultra-critical, live filming presentations. Are you prepared with a wired microphone nearby, all plugged in and ready to swap out? Is the cord long enough? When one of our stage lights blew, sparks were flying everywhere just as an entertainment act was being introduced.

Our DJ mixer has shit the bed in the middle of a really amazing set. From level ten to level zero energy in a flash; that sucked ass. Our beer cooler decided to pass not so quietly into the smoky afterlife during a really crowded event. That wasn't the end of it. Our fire and smoke alarms went off and were loud enough to wake the dead within a two-block radius. Which also shuts down the AC system. That was fun (not). Another time, early on in my career, the cops showed up to investigate violations of the city's noise ordinance. They stopped the band and dancers mid-groove-wiggle.

So much can and will go wrong. Still, for those of us who are true troopers, we just "carry on," as the British like to say. We smile and keep moving forward. #NoFear. #GetYourHandsUpAndFIGHT

I traveled to Kiev and Odessa in Ukraine back in 2008 and learned firsthand about the unreliability of electrical power. When we went out exploring, clubbing, and such—which was every night—the power would suddenly go out from time to time. A few minutes or hours would pass, and, zip, it came back on. The natives never seemed to care. It was part of their daily routine. In fact, they offered a round of free shots and had those candles out and lit lickety-split. They turned the tables on their misfortunes and found the silver lining, as we all should.

 Speaking of shots, they had this incredible five-layer shot that I'll never forget. It took several minutes to make and less than that to knock me flat. No matter how you spell it: Na zdorov'ya, Na Zdorovie, and Nostrovia!

Take a lesson from me. In worst-case scenarios, like Irma, the 2017 hurricane that passed over and around Florida, all you really needed, aside from guests, were some candles and booze. Music helps a lot. If you've invited the right mix of peeps, then someone will emerge who can carry a tune and sing. Maybe my most delightful pal, Amanda Jaay, the gorgeous and oh-so-talented Mayven Missbehavin, will be there. She lights up a room. Remember the importance of inviting the right people to your event? Understand that when all else fails, it's candles (or fire), and your guests that can become the essential ingredients for a great party. (Party favors, like booze and cannabis, certainly come in handy.)

Life can be bitter and sweet. There may be no "perfect event" in the mind of every guest, but that doesn't mean your events can't be perfect for you and your memories. On the day of a big event, I always take deep breaths in and out. I relax and enjoy myself. My best advice is to smile, have a drink after the event has started, and enjoy the fact that no matter what happens tonight, you deserve a pat on the back. Of course, my most important advice is to follow my advice. (Which includes me. Ha!)

I mentioned that we recently survived the biggest hurricane (Irma) on record. She had sustained winds of 185 miles per hour. Irma crushed Puerto Rico, the Virgin Islands, and was headed straight for NOVA and my hometown, St. Pete. There was zero I could do about it. We all know it's easier to give advice than to receive it, but what I did with Irma was follow my own advice. I relaxed and let it happen. I went to sleep in prison that night—literally—thinking that when I woke up, everything I knew, loved, and owned, could be devastated by morning. I was staying in Boston at the Liberty Hotel, a hundred-year-old prison converted into the most amazing hotel, and even though I slept in prison, I didn't allow my mind to become one. I reminded myself to fix what I could and not worry about the rest because I was just wasting precious time and energy.

I was not looking forward to getting knocked out of business by Irma. Every mortal has limits, and even though I could still hear Amir screaming, "Get your hands up Mike, and fight," one financial knockout in my lifetime was enough. Thankfully, the morning sun shone upon our still-beautiful Tampa and St. Petersburg. We got so, so lucky. #Thankful and #Grateful.

Chapter 16

The Aftermath

Where am I? I wake with a start, my head blurry, sunlight pouring into the room.

"Where is my fucking cell phone?"

During a frantic search, I smile, recalling how epic last night was. Wow, what time is it now? Grabbing my shirt, I don't recognize the color of lipstick all over it.

Ugh, my head hurts. Hydrate, hydrate, hydrate. Did I drink at least one bottle of water after every other drink? Umm, did I forget my own words of wisdom? Did I forget to eat lunch and then wolf down two huge pieces of thick-icing cake off the bakery platter just before the event? And then, did I follow that up with a mouthful of mints at midnight? I did not. But maybe you did. And that's why you feel like shit right now.

Let's see. . . . Do you remember who's supposed to be picking up the stage? And all those piles of stacked chairs? Your head is pounding, and you'd like to call somebody, except you can't find your stupid phone. Where is your wedding ring, anyway? Anyone need a bail bondsman?

OMG. I wonder what's been posted on social media. Where are my wallet, cell phone, and wedding ring? That video of you and your boss's heavy-hitter friends dancing and killing that bottle of whiskey at 4:48 AM might not be as entertaining at 4:48 PM the next day when one of their boardroom colleagues gets an alert on their smartphone to check it out. Where is my phone? Oh, how YouTube and a 100-inch 4K TV can come back to bite your (now ex) best friend's funny video. You consider whether you need to be thinking about a career change. (I met a guy on Easter Island who is looking for a reliable bar-back. Ha!)

Of course, you have these moments of terror. These are the times that make you feel truly alive. It's like a near-auto-collision on the freeway. You swerve at the last second as your car fishtails, avoiding death just in the nick of time. The next thing you know, your heart is leaping into your throat. You feel the pounding of an adrenaline surge. Thank goodness you're still alive.

That's the aftermath of a great party. You worry if you're missing an earring or bracelet, but then you remember that your Uber driver was cute. She was low on gas, so you all swung into the gas station that unfortunately had a liquor store and western bar attached. Did you really go in with her for just one more? OMG. Then you all stopped by the beach because the moon was so full and beautiful. Moonlight selfies on the beach? Holy Shit. Did you post your photos after that early-morning swim when she double-dog-dared you? You find the receipt from Busters Beatdown Liquor Store and Bar: a 1.75 Cougano strength spiced rum, a 64 oz. cola-Slurpee, and some rolling papers. What the hell did you do? Haha!

You vaguely recall a double-length, professionally rolled blunt and those incredible edible gummy bears. Where are your keys? Oh shit. You just remembered singing, "What Do You Do for Money Honey" (AC/DC) instead of finishing your keynote speech. Shouldn't have had that tequila shot at noon. What's Grandma going to say when she sees you at her Sunday dinner next week?

Parties and events are the medicine our sick, over-worked, overstressed society needs. The natives need to let off steam. A lot of steam. Events and parties are safe places that make us feel like it's okay to let our proverbial hair down (sometimes literally).

The event was a great tension reliever for your guests. We all need to relax, enjoy, let go, and go wild now and then because we all wear masks. We have our professional masks that define us: plumber, salesman, or event planner. We tend to wear our masks with our friends, even within relationships. We all—well, except for those super-evolved and enlightened Gandhi-beings—pretend a bit. And if we aren't exercising, meditating, traveling, having enough sex, etc., then stress builds up like steam pressure. It needs to be released somehow.

Events and parties are enjoyable ways for us to remove our masks, have a few martinis or some hits on your friend's vape, find yourself on stage, drink in hand, maybe kissing that band's cute lead singer. She's alluring, no doubt. Next, you're screaming some barely coherent words into a microphone. Yet, during those moments, you are alive.

Isn't it great? You are thrilled and enjoying yourself, jumping for joy. All that pent-up stress, rage, loneliness, anxiety, fear, angst, and frustrations miraculously melt away. If you can imagine it, picture me on a dance floor doing my infamous pterodactyl/chicken/seagull dance moves. Yes, it's a thing, and it's hilarious. People laugh at me and with me because I'm fearless, free, and alive, and really, for these precious moments, I just don't give a *fuck*. These moments are worth all the money spent, all the planning, logistical headaches, and cleanup. They're worth it all.

For me, a guy who throws event after event after event—over 2,000 of them by now—it's about seeing people that I love. Relaxing, talking, singing, or dancing. Those moments, when most of the stiffs have left, and the party was supposed to have ended, yet no one who's still there wants to leave. I savor those rare moments, and I watch them linger.

These 5:00 AM moments are too precious. They're the moments when we are breathing rarified air and feeling alive.

These are moments when the CEOs and VPs who stressed all month about their big speech or presentation in front of hundreds of people are all done. Whew! You can see the relief bloom on their faces. Their PowerPoint may have had a wrong slide, their video's sound may have been bad, but that's all in the past. They can now, masks removed—tasks, schedules, and calendars momentarily forgotten—enjoy their vino, scotch, cigar, or whatever. It's nice to see them smiling, laughing, and connecting with their fellow humans. Masks are temporarily removed. CEOs and entry-level college grads mingling together with the bar-backs and catering crew as one. Laughing, singing, dancing, and enjoying themselves. As humanity should.

To me, this the greatest thank-you I get. I love seeing people truly enjoying themselves and letting go. I do my best to make that my gift. Leaving the lights low, alcohol bar sales are closed by 3:00 AM, and my team is completing their EON processes. People are calling for rideshares, trying to hook-up with the old school friend, "sure, I'll drive you home," or whatever. Occasionally, someone is too fucked up to even do that. I'll call them a rideshare on my own account and send them home. Hopefully, it's only a twenty-dollar ride, but either way, it's the right thing to do personally and professionally. And sometimes, they are so hammered and annoying that I'm happy to spend twenty dollars just to get them safely home.

So, when you're scrambling to find your Visa card, your earring, your phone, and your dignity, remember these moments you feel alive. Pat yourself on the back. You're a successful party planner or newlywed bride or groom. Your guests appreciate your energy, schmoozing, dancing, singing, silliness, antics, whatever. Venues, homes, and buildings are just empty rooms without you and your energy. Bravo to you!

I thank people all the time for coming to NOVA because without them supporting our events, like our annual NOVAween party or weekly Entrepreneur Social Club, it would just be me standing alone in an empty building. This industry, the event world, is about marrying (haha) the best venue with the right group of people. And filling that space with love and laughs, oddity, and silliness, some wild cards, and—oh shit, look at Lisa coming back with Steve. She's got that wild look in her eyes and a rat's nest of fuck-me hair. Wow. Never expected those two to hook up tonight. They usually hate each other, but, hey, it's what we do in the event world.

With that, I'll leave you now. Enjoy your event planning and remember to have fun with it. Until next time, when we gather to share some of that precious air, full of life, in those delightfully rare moments, just before we hear someone off in the distance, yelling, "It's 5 AM Go Home!"

Or maybe I heard, "It's 5 AM What's Next?"

Acknowledgements

Special thanks to my old-school core of costumed fellow Halloween "NOVAween" freakers: David Hoang, Joe Costa, Ed and Danny Pugliese, Chris Goodall, Alexis Winning, Lou Garcia, Jesse Battle, Dean Shafer, Drew and Helene Edwards, Chris Novilla, Julie Schultz, Mikey Ruggieri, Jakub Kulakowski, Deb Siegel, Keith "Hippie" O'Loughlin, Amir and Farrah Ardebily, Amy Miller, Gia Porras, Scott Shirah, Chris and Kelley Skeie, T and K Nesbitt, Chris 'Ragger' Wolverton, Frank Revello, Will and Jacquelyn Caban, Marlene Sundquist, Melissa Nguyen and Ruby Thomas Dolce, The Aljasir Brothers: Jon, Jamil and Amil, Christy and Steve Brown, Cousin Rod MacKenzie and Colleen, Brian "Ling Ling" Nelson, Bert and Colleen Novilla, and my fabulous neighbor and real-estate guru, John Barkett. All whose love and energy are shared here at NOVA 535 has created the most magical of our annual events! Extra hugs and love for my fellow visionary, the incredible Marina Williams, owner of Art Pool.

Marina, along with 5-Star help from her mom Becky, and her partner Evan, for always helping me create such magical Halloween costumes.

Thanks to a true healer, Dr. James O'Neil, for keeping me healthy, properly aligned, and with a clearer understanding of how my body works.

Once again, thank you, Momma and Dad (RIP), for giving me life and leading me by such a good example.

I love you all.

Michael Scott Novilla
June 1, 2019

About the Author

Born on April Fools' Day in St. Pete, Florida, Michael Scott Novilla has always loved learning, exploring, and making things better. Since completing his MBA in 1993, he has bought, renovated, and leased over one hundred historic buildings. Along the way, he realized his hometown deserved a unique event space, so he built a world-class venue called NOVA 535, which he has run since 2008.

In 2009, needing the company of like-minded folks, he created the Entrepreneur Social Club, a network of business owners from around the world who meet every

Thursday to collaborate, mentor, and share knowledge. Now, traveling around the world (87 countries and counting), he is using the expertise he has gained from throwing over two thousand 5-star weddings, parties, and events to consult with business owners worldwide, showing them how to achieve world-class service and operations in their business.

His first book "It's 5 AM Go Home!" is a hilarious, step-by-step guide to throwing your own amazing 5-star parties and events.

MichaelSNovilla.com

CPSIA information can be obtained
at www.ICGtesting.com
Printed in the USA
FSHW010615261019
63403FS